Egyptian Mythology for Teens

Enthralling Myths from Ancient Egypt

© Copyright 2025 - All rights reserved.

The content contained within this book may not be reproduced, duplicated, or transmitted without direct written permission from the author or the publisher.

Under no circumstances will any blame or legal responsibility be held against the publisher, or author, for any damages, reparation, or monetary loss due to the information contained within this book, either directly or indirectly.

Legal Notice:

This book is copyright protected. It is only for personal use. You cannot amend, distribute, sell, use, quote, or paraphrase any part, or the content within this book, without the consent of the author or publisher.

Disclaimer Notice:

Please note the information contained within this document is for educational and entertainment purposes only. All effort has been executed to present accurate, up-to-date, reliable, and complete information. No warranties of any kind are declared or implied. Readers acknowledge that the author is not engaging in the rendering of legal, financial, medical, or professional advice. The content within this book has been derived from various sources. Please consult a licensed professional before attempting any techniques outlined in this book.

By reading this document, the reader agrees that under no circumstances is the author responsible for any losses, direct or indirect, that are incurred as a result of the use of the information contained within this document, including, but not limited to, errors, omissions, or inaccuracies.

Free limited time bonus

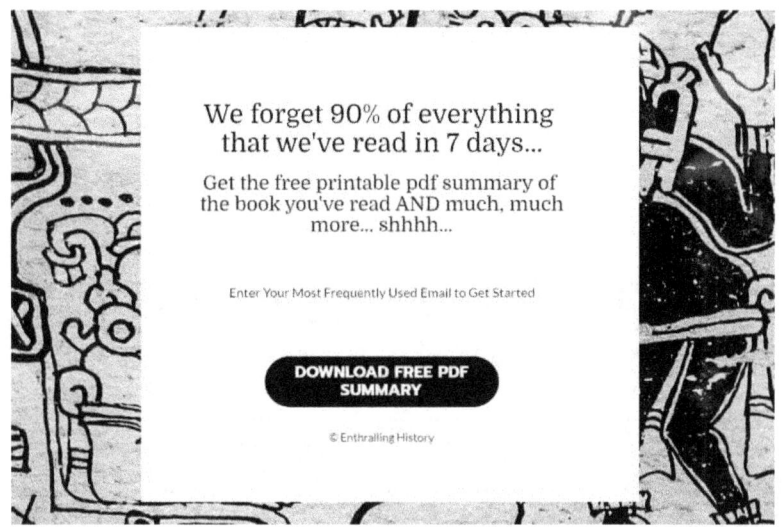

Stop for a moment. We have a free bonus set up for you. The problem is this: we forget 90% of everything that we read after 7 days. Crazy fact, right? Here's the solution: we've created a printable, 1-page pdf summary for this book that you're reading now. All you have to do to get your free pdf summary is to go to the following website: https://livetolearn.lpages.co/enthrallinghistory/

Or, Scan the QR code!

Once you do, it will be intuitive. Enjoy, and thank you!

Table of Contents

INTRODUCTION 1
PRONUNCIATION OF CHIEF EGYPTIAN GODS AND GODDESSES 4
CHAPTER 1: EGYPTIAN COSMOLOGY 5
CHAPTER 2: THE SUN GOD RA 16
CHAPTER 3: THE EGYPTIAN PANTHEON 26
CHAPTER 4: THE OSIRIS MYTH 40
CHAPTER 5: ISIS AND THE SCORPION MYTHS 51
CHAPTER 6: TALES FROM DUAT (THE UNDERWORLD) 61
CHAPTER 7: THE PHARAOH'S CURSE 75
CHAPTER 8: THE SPHINX AND OTHER MONSTERS 86
CHAPTER 9: MYTHS OF JUSTICE AND LOVE 96
CHAPTER 10: MYTHS OF MAIDENS AND MAGICIANS 107
ANSWER KEY TO ROUNDUP ACTIVITIES 114
HERE'S ANOTHER BOOK BY ENTHRALLING HISTORY THAT YOU MIGHT LIKE 119
FREE LIMITED TIME BONUS 120
BIBLIOGRAPHY 121
IMAGE SOURCES 123

Introduction

When did the Nile begin flowing? Who created the cheetahs, hippos, and crocodiles? What happens when we die? Why does good and evil exist? Who is controlling the world?

The ancient Egyptians wondered about these questions and many more. Their mythology was a collection of tales that decoded life's mysteries, handed down over the generations. Egyptian mythology explained creation, people's relationship with the supernatural, and the values that informed their attitudes and actions.

Mythology helped the Egyptians make sense of their world. Where did the sun go at night? It must be a god, right? It brings light and warmth. Surely, it must be the greatest god! But who made the sun? That god must be even more wonderful!

Egypt emerged as an advanced civilization around the same time as Sumer in ancient Iraq. These civilizations even interacted with each other. However, the Sumerians and Egyptians had different spins on how everything came to be or even what the gods looked like. Sumerian gods looked like people, while Egyptian gods often had animal heads and human bodies. Sometimes, an Egyptian god had a body that combined three animals, like a crocodile, a hippopotamus, and a lioness.

The Egyptian beliefs about the supernatural affected every part of their lives. They strove for harmony with each other because they believed that conflict weighed the heart down. A heavy heart would not make it into the afterlife. Husbands and wives worked hard at relationship skills because they thought they would be married to each other throughout eternity. They believed their pharaoh was a living representation of a god, so they dared not rebel or cast shade on him.

When the Nile didn't flood as it should, and the crops failed, the Egyptians assumed they must have offended a god. When something good happened, it meant the gods were smiling down on them. If the Egyptians had a problem, their mythology helped them understand why and what to do. For instance, they thought demons caused migraines and other issues, so they needed to know the magic spells to cast them out.

Egyptian mythology evolved, and the old gods changed. The Egyptians blended gods, like the creator Atum and the sun god Ra. They added new gods in.

As this book discusses various aspects of Egyptian mythology, it will mention different periods in ancient Egypt. An Egyptian priest named Manetho organized Egypt's history into thirty ***dynasties***. A dynasty was a period when all the kings (and a few queens) descended from the same family. When that family ran out of heirs or was overthrown, a new dynasty began.

Modern historians divided ancient Egypt into three major "kingdoms" or "golden ages." In these times, Egypt's kings were powerful, new and exciting things were happening, and Egypt was rolling in wealth. Each "kingdom" had several dynasties. When things fell apart, Egypt had chaotic intermediate periods until the next kingdom arose. No one quite agrees on when the three kingdoms began and ended because the ancient Egyptians tracked time by the reign of a king. They would say, "In the second year of king so-and-so, this and that happened." Ancient Egyptian dates are a rough guess!

- Predynastic (4300-3100 BCE)
- Early Dynastic (3100 - 2700 BCE)
- Old Kingdom 2700 - 2200 BCE
- Middle Kingdom 2040 - 1760 BCE
- New Kingdom 1550 - 1100 BCE

One point of reading history is understanding how the past influences us today. We will encounter bizarre stories while reading through ancient Egypt's mythology. They might seem light years away from our belief systems today. Yet, we may find points of contact or stories with a familiar ring. Mythology impacts values, and we will likely uncover some ancient Egyptian values that resonate. While reading this book, think about why those values were essential to the Egyptians and why they are still important today.

Pronunciation of Chief Egyptian Gods and Goddesses

Amun: *ah-men*
Ra: *rah*
Osiris (Usir): *oo-seer*
Isis: *ee-set*
Nephthys: *neb-et-hut*
Set/Seth: *set*
Horus: *hor*
Maat: *meh-aht*
Hathor: *hat-hor*
Nut: *nit*
Geb: *gib*

Chapter 1: Egyptian Cosmology

What is *cosmology*? It tells us how the universe came to be and how it developed. It's an effort to understand our universe and how everything fits together. This chapter will jump into the ancient Egyptian concept of cosmology. How did the Egyptians explain what they could see in our galaxy?

The Egyptians knew their understanding of cosmology was obscure. Much of it was a mystery beyond knowing. Nevertheless, what the Egyptians did understand about cosmology placed them ahead of most civilizations of their day. They tracked the sun and the moon moving through the sky. They developed maps of constellations with lists of the stars. They used their observations of the sun and moon to create a 365-day calendar. They wove their knowledge of the cosmos into the core of their mythology, trying to explain how it all came into being.

What Was the Egyptian Creation Myth?

So, who was the Egyptian creator and how did the ancient Egyptians believe he created the world? The ancient Egyptians had several myths about creation depending on the city they lived in. Ancient Egypt was not a unified country in its earliest days. Several cities arose to rule the area around them. These city-states developed their own ideas about cosmology and religion. They often disagreed on who did the creating. However, all the myths had common elements, like the dark waters before creation. Later, when Egypt unified (only to split up again several times), some of the ancient cities clung to their myths. Others blended their ideas with those from other places.

One of Egypt's oldest religious centers was Heliopolis, near today's Cairo. Its version of the creation myth began with the god Atum, also identified as Amun, especially in the New Kingdom. Sometimes, the Egyptians combined him with the sun god, calling him Atum-Re or Amun-Ra.

In the beginning, everything was dark and covered by the primeval, chaotic ocean of Nun. Then, Atum pulled a pyramid-shaped island called the ***benben*** out of the water. Standing on the island, he spat, forming Shu, god of the air. Then he vomited (or sneezed), creating the lioness-headed Tefnut, goddess of the rain and moisture. Shu and Tefnut gave birth to Geb, god of the earth, and Nut, goddess of the sky.

Tefnut, mother of earth and sky [1]

The Cosmic Egg: Another Version of Creation

Hermopolis was a city in Middle Egypt and another sacred center. Its original name was Khemnu, meaning "Eight-Town." This name came from its creation myth that began with a group of eight deities called the Ogdoad. The four goddesses had snake heads, and the four gods had frog heads. They formed four pairs. Nun and Naunet were the god and goddess of the water. Heh and Hauhet were the deities of infinite chaos. Kek and Kauket were the god and goddess of darkness. Amun and Amaunet were the deities of invisibility or hiddenness.

Together, these eight deities represented a dark, watery, hidden chaos. The energy produced between these deities created an intense explosion, the Egyptian version of the Big Bang. Then the benben (pyramid-shaped island) rose out of the sea. The first period of the earth began—the Golden Age-ruled by the eight deities of the Ogdoad.

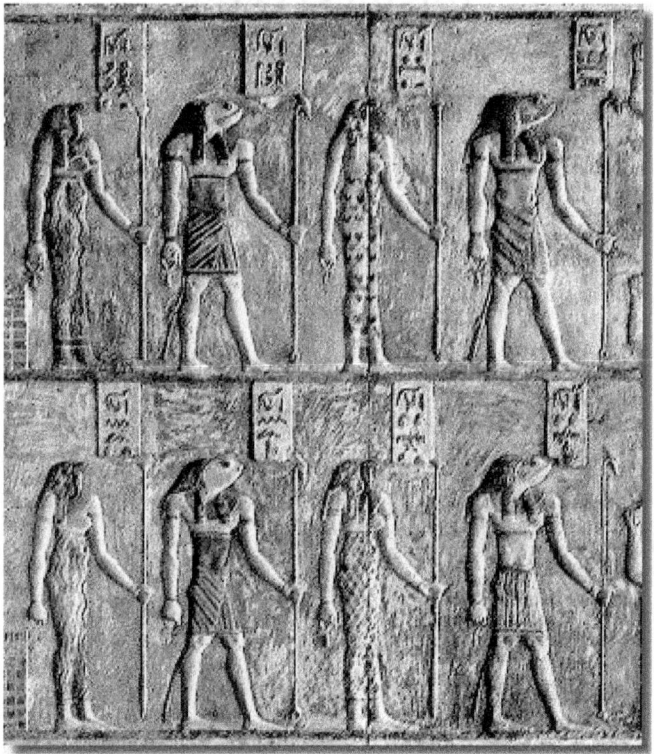

The Ogdoad[2]

These eight primeval deities produced a cosmic egg. Here, the story has several variations. One says the gods themselves created it. Another is that the *Great Cackler*, a primeval goose, laid the egg. Who created the goose, and when? The story doesn't explain. The sun god Ra hatched from the egg and created everything else. With the sun came light and life. A variation of the egg story is that it wasn't laid by a goose but by a sacred ibis bird. The ibis was Thoth, the god of science, magic, and writing.

In Thebes, a city in southern Egypt that served as its capital for some time, the people followed the Ogdoad myth with the egg but said Amun was the supreme god and different from Atum. They said Amun created the other seven gods of the Ogdoad and the island Atum stood on. He also created the Great Cackler goose, which laid the egg Ra hatched from.

A Lotus Flower and a Poop Bug—Yet Another Spin on Creation

Another version from Hermopolis doesn't involve an egg but a lotus flower, which grew up through the dark waters of chaos. As its petals slowly opened, a bird of light burst forth. It was Ra, the sun god. A variation of the lotus flower story is that a scarab beetle, not Ra, came out of the flower and turned into a boy named Nefertum. When he cried, his tears made the first humans.

What is a scarab beetle? It's a dung beetle. It goes looking for poop, makes balls of it, and rolls the balls back to its nest for its newly hatched babies to eat.

The ancient Egyptians thought the balls of poop represented our world, and it was the beetle's duty to roll it along, keeping it turning on its axis. The Egyptians revered this humble beetle for its part in the cycle of life and its role in creation. They made seals in the shape of the scarab beetle to sign their names. Egyptians wore these dung-beetle-shaped seals on rings, so they were always handy.

A scarab beetle seal on a ring[3]

Who Was Ptah?

Memphis, which sits across the Nile and slightly south of Thebes, was another of Egypt's capitals several times in history. While the other versions of the creation story had common elements, the Memphis version had a completely different god as the creator. His name was Ptah, and he created everything with his words: he spoke the word, and the world came into existence. He also created the other gods. In addition to being the creator, he was the god of artisans and architects. An ancient hymn said, "He crafted the world in the design of his heart." Ptah was also the god of eternity, truth, and justice. In paintings, he usually had green skin and wore a shroud. However, he was sometimes portrayed as a deformed dwarf.

The Great Rebellion: The Tale of the Heavenly Cow

Atum-Ra created men from his tears. But after thousands of years, humans began to laugh at him because he was so old. How could he run the world at his age? When Atum-Ra heard about their rebellion, he seethed with rage and called a council of the other gods. Nun, the goddess of the chaotic ocean, spoke up: "Send your Eye to destroy the humans!"

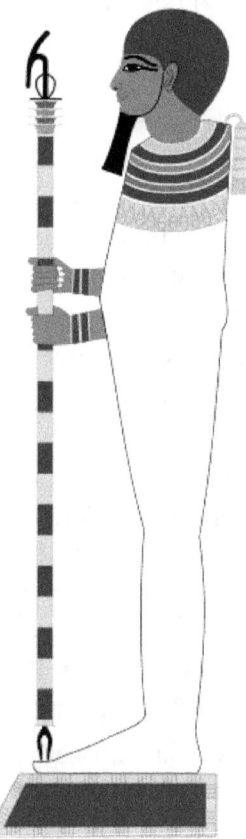

Ptah, the creator[4]

The Eye of Ra was Hathor. Like a lioness, she was the fiercest of the goddesses. She began wiping out the human race until almost everyone died. She laughed as she killed people, a terrible sound like the growls of a lioness tearing her prey. The rivers ran red with the blood of men and women.

When he saw the devastation, Atum-Ra's anger turned to pity. He commanded Hathor to stop her killing spree. However, the ruthless goddess was enjoying drinking the blood of her victims. She refused to obey.

"Quick! Messengers, go to Heliopolis and get the red fruit that causes sleep," Atum-Ra commanded. His messengers rushed off like a blast of wind. In Heliopolis, the women crushed barley and made 7,000 jars of beer. They dyed the beer red with the crimson juice of the red fruit. Ra inspected their work and was pleased.

"It looks like blood!" he said approvingly. "We will use this to save the humans. Pour it on the plains of Dendera."

When Hathor saw the beer flooding the plain, she thought it was blood and drank it all. The more she drank, the more she laughed. Finally, she was so drunk she couldn't stand. The red fruit and beer had made her too sleepy to think.

Ra came up and put his arm around her. "Come with me in peace, sweet one. It's time for you to sleep."

When she awoke, Hathor had changed back into the peaceful friend of humans. Yet, the damage was done. Creation was fractured. Now, the world had suffering and death. Harmony, order, and balance were lost.

But, you might be thinking, why is the story called the "Tale of the Heavenly Cow?" Ra was sick and tired of ruling the world. "I've had enough of these ungrateful humans!" he said. "Shu, you take my place here. You're in charge of the world. Nut, carry me to the highest heavens! I want to go rest there."

"Sir," Nut protested, "I don't know how to do that!"

So, Ra transformed Nut, the sky goddess, into a heavenly cow. She carried him on her back to the heavens, leaving the other gods to manage the disorderly humans.

Nut, the heavenly cow[5]

The humans weren't the only rebels. Before the fall of man, Ra had given express orders to Nut and the earth-god Geb. "Sky and earth, you're spending too much time together! Don't start having children. We have enough gods around here!"

"Shu!" Ra barked to the god of the atmosphere. "You're supposed to be between the sky and earth. Keep them separated!"

But Shu couldn't keep the couple apart, and Nut got pregnant. So, Ra laid down the law to Nut: "You can't give birth on any day in the calendar year!"

At that time, the calendar year was 360 days with twelve months. Each month was thirty days. What was Nut to do with these babies she was carrying?

Thoth, the god of wisdom, had a plan to help Nut. He challenged Khonsu, the moon god, to a gambling match. Khonsu kept losing and had to give Thoth some of his moonlight. Finally, Thoth collected enough moonlight to make five more days in the year. He gave those days to Nut, and she had a baby on each of those five extra days. That's why we now have 365 days in our year, according to Egyptian mythology.

Nut gave birth to Osiris, Isis, Set (Seth), Nephthys, and Horus the Elder. The heavenly battle between good and evil, which we will unwrap later, began between these siblings. Ra had warned Nut, and she didn't listen. That's why Ra had Nut go with him to the highest heavens. He separated her and Geb forever. Geb's bitter tears became the rain and oceans.

What Did the Ancient Egyptians Think the Milky Way Was?

Have you ever been far away from any city and looked up into the night sky? If it was a clear night, you probably saw the hazy band of light that is our Milky Way galaxy. It's actually a disk, but since we're inside that disk, we see a stretch of light behind dark streaks and patches. Sometimes, the dark area looks like a dragon or a collection of spider webs. Imagine what it was like to look into the night sky 4,000 years ago when electric lights were non-existent. Without this "light pollution," it caught the attention of most ancient civilizations. Almost all cultures wove the Milky Way into their mythology.

In the earlier eras of ancient Egypt, people wondered what happened to the sun when it set at night. They decided that the sky goddess Nut swallowed the sun, and then it passed through her body during the night and came back out at sunrise. They thought the Milky Way was Nut, with the sun brightening her body as it passed through. Later, the Egyptians believed that the sun passed into the underworld and back into the present world in the morning.

What Was "Maat?" How Did It Affect the Order of the Universe?

Perhaps we should ask, *who* was Maat? Maat was both a goddess and a concept. The goddess Maat was the daughter of the sun god Ra. She represented the concepts of Maat: balance, harmony, and justice. For the Egyptians, Maat was divine order. This order affected everything in the natural world.

The goddess Maat[6]

The ancient Egyptians believed that the creator formed a world with order and meaning. He created a world of plenty where all people and animals had everything they needed. However, the world and its people fell from the creator's intended order. When they rebelled against Ra, they disrupted Maat. The Egyptians used the word *Isfet* to describe the "lack" or suffering that creation experienced when its order fell apart. This lack of Maat caused all evil things, like sickness, death, poverty, injustice, and war. The Egyptians worked hard to restore the Maat, or the order, they had lost. Maat brought justice, peace, and harmony. When Maat was restored, the world and its people had everything they needed.

Why Was the Pharaoh So Important in Maintaining Order in the World?

Egypt's king led the activities meant to restore Maat, aided by the priests. Yet, everyone participated in carrying out Maat. Two divine powers accompanied the creator: *Sia* (the ability to see) and *Hu* (the ability to speak). The king could "see" Maat, keep it in his heart, and speak it out. When he spoke it out, Maat became a reality.

Maat brought abundance, and the pharaoh's role was to distribute that abundance fairly so that everyone had enough. In his worship, the pharaoh presented to Ra a world that was orderly and cared for. The king demonstrated to the creator that he was maintaining Maat.

What were the king's primary duties to restore and maintain Maat?

1. He ensured justice for all people and enough of what they needed.
2. He kept the gods happy by offering sacrifices to them and to his forefathers who had died. (The kings became gods when they died.)
3. He defended Egypt from invaders or other nations that threatened the country's well-being.
4. He restored and maintained the order of creation by issuing laws for an orderly society.

The Egyptians considered their king's laws to represent the creator's will. The king had to set a good example by following these laws himself. He also had to enforce the laws for everyone in Egypt to keep harmony and justice. Inscriptions said the pharaoh "put Maat in the place of injustice." The king, his vizier (prime minister), and the supreme courts made legal decisions and judgments on crimes against Egypt's government or royalty. The vizier was the chief priest of Maat and the high judge in the courts.

What About Everyone Else? What Did People Need to Do to Restore Maat?

Everyone had to do their best to be fair and impartial. Because of this effort, their sense of justice was well-developed compared to other societies of the time. Everyone knew that taking the law into their own hands was counterproductive. If they had a dispute, they relied on fair treatment in the court system. It was okay to advocate for one's rights. Yet, advocating for another person's rights was a powerful way to restore Maat.

Maat affected all aspects of peoples' lives and their understanding of cosmology. They believed that maintaining Maat decided what happened to them after they died. They tried their hardest to live in harmony with everyone else. For the ancient Egyptians, balance and cooperation were the driving forces in their lives. Conflict with others affected the order in the cosmos.

How Did Ancient Egyptian Temples Replicate the Universe?

Egyptian temples were places to worship the gods, yet they built them as replicas of the universe when Atum-Ra created it. He pulled the island out of the dark sea of chaos and stood on its hill, calling other things into existence. The inner sanctuaries of ancient Egyptian temples represented the benben (primeval mound). As a person walked into the center of a temple to the holiest place, the floor gradually rose higher, and the ceiling lowered. The inner courts had no windows, so it was dark, like the days of creation before the sun was created. As the priests moved through the shadowlands of the inner temple, it transported them to the beginning of time.

Chapter 1 Activity

Match the name on the left to its definition on the right. You can check your answers in the back of the book.

1. Benben   A. Eight Deities of Creation

2. Geb   B. Eye of Ra

3. Great Cackler   C. God of the earth

4. Hathor   D. Goddess of the sky and the heavenly cow

5. Maat   E. Goddess (and concept) of cosmic order

6. Nun   F. Goose that laid the cosmic egg

7. Nut   G. Island that rose out of the water at creation

8. Ogdoad   H. Primeval, chaotic ocean

Chapter 2: The Sun God Ra

In Egypt's hot desert climate, clouds rarely obscure the sun. It shines brightly, day after day. Although it brings searing heat, with temperatures soaring over 100 Fahrenheit in summer, the sun also brings light and life. For the ancient Egyptians, the sun and its personification, the sun god Ra, were central to their mythology. Many Egyptian myths said Ra (or Re) was one of the first gods to be created. Other myths said he *was* the creator and lumped him in with Atum or Amun as the supreme god in Egypt.

What Was the Boat of a Million Years?

The ancient Egyptians thought Ra represented the sun's power, riding his solar barque (a kind of boat) across the heavens. In the daytime, Ra sailed the "Boat of a Million Years" through the sky, shining his light on the world. It was a stunning boat adorned with amethyst, emeralds, jasper, lapis lazuli, and turquoise. At sunset, he disappeared over the horizon into ***Duat***, the underworld. His boat, now called the "Ship of a Million Souls," was stripped of its splendor. It sailed through Duat and came out on the other side at sunrise.

The ***Pyramid Texts*** (2345-2200 BCE) were inscriptions carved into the inside walls of pyramids, giving instructions to a dead king on his journey to Duat. The Pyramid Texts said that Ra would gather the king's soul and sail him to the ***Field of Reeds***, the Egyptian idea of paradise. The Pyramid Texts describe Ra as the supreme god of order and harmony who comforts the souls of the recent dead. Tomb art pictured

Ra with a ram head standing in the middle of the golden boat with the serpent god Mehen coiled in an arch over him.

Ra on his golden barque⁷

Who Was Apep? Why Did Ra Fight Him Every Night?

Ra's soul separated from his body at the entrance to Duat. The two remained separated until his soul came out on the other side at sunrise. On his journey through Duat, he took on the appearance of Osiris, god of the underworld. Ra sailed through twelve sections of Duat, representing the twelve hours of the night. The first section wasn't entirely dark, as six coiled fire-breathing serpents lined each side of the river. Ra sailed on, encountering disastrous forces, demons, and devious gods. Yet, the good gods helped him defeat these horrors and rise on the horizon in the morning.

In the first section, representing sunset, a smaller boat held a scarab beetle, representing the cycle of life. The goddess Maat guided Ra in an orderly way through the chaos of Duat. As the night progressed, Ra sailed through the dark waters of the primeval goddess Nun. When he entered the darker part of Duat, the land on either side of the river was a lifeless desert. With outspread wings and raised crests on their heads, multi-headed dragons writhed and hissed. Yet, they let Ra pass through without harm.

As Ra sailed on, the river wound through a deep ravine, with steep walls rising on either side. This region was the "Mouth of the Tomb." Here, Ra's boat transformed into a serpent with glittering scales and poisonous fangs. Ra passed over the Lake of Fire, which could consume or refresh the dead. Souls in torment screamed out to him from the fiery waters, but they had no hope. They had sealed their fate with their rebellious lives.

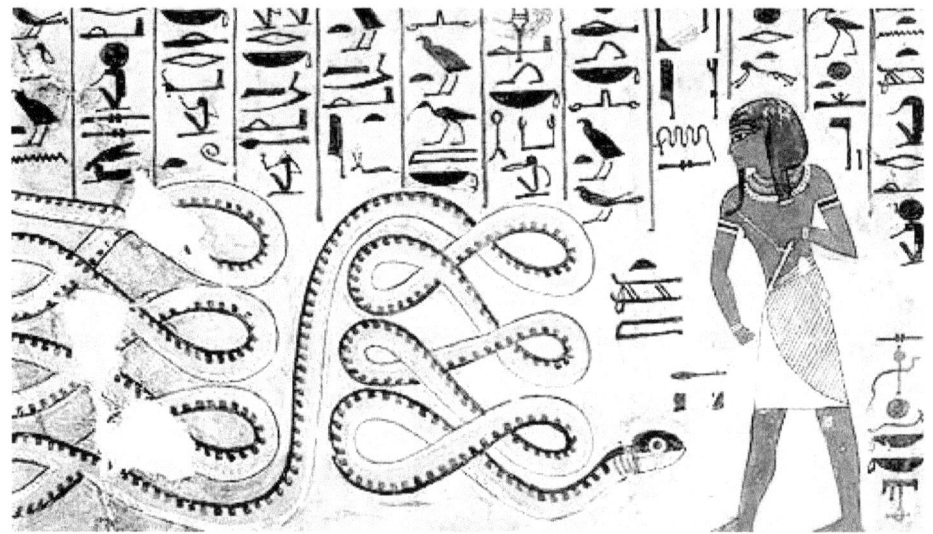

Apep attacked Ra each night.[8]

In the darkest hour of the night, a place of horror and dismay, Apep, the terrifying snake god of chaos, lay waiting for him in the "secret cavern." Apep tried to keep Ra from continuing his journey. If Ra never made it out of Duat, the sun would not rise, and all life on earth would die. Every night, Apep swallowed the waters of Nun, attempting to run the golden barque aground.

Osiris's sister-wife, Isis, used her magical incantations to keep the boat moving along. The guardian serpent, Mehen, who traveled with Ra, wrapped his coils around Ra, protecting him. Apep roared like thunder, yet he was powerless against Isis's spell.

As sunrise approached, Ra passed through the "Sarcophagus of the Gods." In this mysterious place, the dead gods rested, wrapped up as mummies. They called out greetings to Ra, but the chasm between them and Ra was so broad that their voices sounded like buzzing bees.

Then, the portals of Duat flung open, and Ra finally made his way back up to the mortal world. Osiris's son, Horus, commanded a serpent to unleash the unquenchable fire on the enemies of Osiris and Ra. Ra was reborn as Khepri, the scarab beetle god, at sunrise.

What Were Ra's Attributes and Powers?

Ra was the god of life, transformation, and order. Just as the sun transformed seeds into grain, fruit, and vegetables, the Egyptians believed Ra could transform situations for the better. As he passed through Duat each night, he triumphed over chaos and restored order to the world. Therefore, the Egyptians depended on him to resolve turmoil and bring harmony. Ra was the father of Maat, the goddess who represented balance and order.

In the early days of creation, Atum-Ra ruled directly over people as their first pharaoh. He gave laws to humans. But after they rebelled, he left them for the highest heavens. Atum-Ra still controlled the world in a more distant, unapproachable way. He continued as the ultimate power behind the other gods and the patron of the pharaohs. The Egyptians called their kings "the son of Ra." The kings built "solar temples" to Ra. These were different from the gloomy, dark temples of other gods. They were open to the sky and had no idols of Ra. They did not need a representation of Ra since he was the sun in the sky.

Ra with a falcon head and sun disk on his head[9]

Why the Falcon Head?

As we saw earlier, in some Egyptian myths, Ra morphed into a scarab beetle when he emerged from the underworld at sunrise. However, other myths say he became a falcon named Horakhty, "Horus of the Horizon." When Ra flew up from the underworld and into the sky in the morning, the Egyptians associated him with Horus, who represented new life.

Whether beetle or falcon, by midday, he had transformed into the sun. Then, in the evening, as the sun set, he took on a ram's head. The ram represented the creator-god Amun, and many Egyptians in the New Kingdom blended Ra with Amun. The Egyptians considered the ram an overcomer. With his horns, a ram could butt his way through obstacles. He was also a sacrificial animal. In a sense, Ra sacrificed himself each night, passing through Duat to bring renewed life to the world.

What About the Solar Disk?

Many paintings or sculptures of Ra show him with a solar disk over his head. The solar disk, called the **Aten**, represented the sun, and many Egyptians believed Ra was the sun. The solar disk was yellow or orange and sometimes had a cobra encircling it. The Egyptians occasionally portrayed the sun disk with wings, which blended in the falcon image representing Horus, son of Isis and Osiris.

Egyptian religion took an unprecedented turn in the New Kingdom under the pharaoh Akhenaten. When his father, Amenhotep III, was king, the worship of Amun was becoming increasingly popular, especially in the capital of Thebes. Amun's identity had merged with Ra (Re) so that he became the creator and king of the gods. The priests of Amun had grown almost as rich and powerful as the pharaoh. Amenhotep no doubt felt threatened by the competing forces of Amun's priests.

Amenhotep III promoted the worship of the Aten, the Solar Disk, as a competitor to Amun-Ra. Instead of mainly worshiping Amun-Ra, who had other identities (creator, chief god), Amenhotep worshiped the "Dazzling Sun Disk" directly. He also worshiped the moon. The Egyptians considered their pharaoh a direct link between them and the gods, so they tended to follow his lead in religious things.

When Amenhotep died and his son, Amenhotep IV, became king, he was even more radical than his father. He changed his name to Akhenaten,

Akhenaten, the radical religious reformer[10]

meaning "Effective for Aten." Akhenaten had a single goal as pharaoh: a revolution in Egypt's religion. He promoted **_monotheism_**, the worship of only one god: the Aten, or Solar Disk. He and his wife (and half-sister) Nefertiti worshiped the Aten and no other gods. This monotheism created quite a stir among the Egyptians, who were used to a vast array of gods.

Akhenaten demanded that temples to other gods be shut down and banned the worship of Amun-Ra and any other god. It was a way of squelching the power of Amun's priests, but for Akhenaten, it also seemed to be a genuine belief. In his hymns, he spoke of the Solar Disk as his loving creator, the maintainer and ruler of the universe, and the one-and-only, all-powerful god. He moved his royal court away from Thebes and the priests of Amun and built a new capital city called Akhetaten (Amarna).

King Tut and his wife under the Solar Disk[11]

After Akhenaten died, his son Tutankhamun became pharaoh at age nine. With the help of his advisors, King Tut restored everything to the way it had been before his father's reign. Amarna lay abandoned, and everyone reverted to **_polytheism_**, the worship of many gods. The priests of Amun reasserted their power from Thebes to the point that they ultimately ruled about two-thirds of Egypt. Amun-Ra was reinstalled as the chief god in Egypt. However, Tutankhamun and his wife, Ankhesenamun, continued to worship the Aten along with all the other gods.

Ra as Khepri, the Dung Beetle

Khepri, the beetle, pushing the sun[12]

As we mentioned, after passing through the underworld, Ra emerged as either a falcon or a scarab beetle named Khepri, depending on the version of the myth. Khepri accompanied Ra on his nighttime journey. How did a humble beetle get associated with the creator god? As we shared earlier, these beetles roll balls of dung to their nest and lay their eggs inside them. When the larvae hatch inside the ball, they eat the poop, grow to about two inches long, then form a pupa (like a cocoon). The Egyptians thought they had been created from nothing when they hatched out of the pupa and crawled out of the ball.

The Egyptians envisioned Khepri the beetle as a manifestation of Ra. They thought of him pushing the sun through the sky in the same way the scarab beetle rolled its ball of poop. However, in Duat, the underworld, Khepri was dead. In the sixth hour of the night, Ra's golden boat came to Khepri's dead body floating on the water.

The beetle was inside the coils of a five-headed snake. As Ra's bodiless soul combined with Khepri's dead body, the scarab beetle resurrected. Ra's boat sailed out of the underworld, with Khepri the beetle at its helm, guiding the voyage. Shu, the god of the atmosphere, assisted Ra-Khepri in their ascent to the sky.

Nem-wer, or the Mnevis Bull[18]

Ra as the Mnevis Bull

An aspect of Ra's soul was Mnevis (Nem-wer), a black bull with a solar disk and a cobra between his horns. His priests in Heliopolis actually had a real bull they considered Mnevis's personification as long as the bull lived. They carefully observed his movements because they thought Ra influenced what the bull did. They believed these movements to be *oracles*, or prophecies of the future. The living bull got two cows as his mates. One represented Hathor, the Eye of Ra, and the other represented Iusaaset, a beetle-headed goddess associated with creation. When the bull died, they embalmed him, buried him in a tomb, and looked for another black bull to take his place.

Ra as the Bennu Bird

In Egyptian mythology, an aspect of Ra's soul was the Bennu bird. He looked like a heron and symbolized rebirth and prosperity. In the Egyptian written language, hieroglyphics, one symbol for Ra was a heron. The Bennu also represented Osiris because Ra assumed the image of Osiris when he entered the underworld each night.

The Bennu bird with the sun disk on its head[14]

The Egyptians thought the Bennu bird created himself out of nothing. They also believed that he recreated himself every once in a while. This reminded them of the sun, which "recreated" itself when it rose each morning. The Egyptians believed Bennu flew over Nun's dark ocean of chaos at creation and landed on a rock. As the bird called out, it determined what creation would be like.

Ra and the Phoenix

The ancient Egyptians associated the legendary phoenix bird with Ra. The fifth-century BCE Greek historian Herodotus wrote about the Egyptian accounts of this spectacular and rare bird. The phoenix had dazzling red and gold feathers and was the size of an eagle. Herodotus said it lived in Arabia. Only one phoenix bird lived at a time and had a lifespan of about 500 years.

When the phoenix realized it would die soon, it built a nest with fragrant tree limbs and spices. It set the nest on fire, and the flames reduced the bird to ashes. However, a new bird rose from the ashes. It rolled its father's ashes into a ball of myrrh and flew with it to Egypt. When it arrived at Ra's Temple of the Sun in Heliopolis, it buried its father there. The Egyptians connected the phoenix to Ra's cycle of death and rebirth as he passed through the underworld each night.

Chapter 2 Activity

Mark each statement with a T or F. Answers are in the back of the book.

( ) 1. Ra's daytime solar barque was called "Boat of a Million Years."

( ) 2. Duat was the Egyptian underworld.

( ) 3. The Tree-covered Mountain was the Egyptian idea of paradise.

( ) 4. Apep was an elephant god.

( ) 5. Some myths say Ra became a scarab beetle at sunrise.

( ) 6. Monotheism is the worship of many gods.

( ) 7. Khepri was a falcon.

( ) 8. The Bennu bird looked like a heron and symbolized rebirth.

( ) 9. The phoenix buried its father at Ra's Temple of the Sun in Heliopolis.

( ) 10. The Egyptians thought Ra influenced the actions of the Mnevis bull.

Chapter 3: The Egyptian Pantheon

What is a *pantheon*? It means "of all gods." It is a group of gods within a belief system. The Egyptian religion was *polytheistic*, with around nine major gods and more than a thousand lesser gods. We've already discussed Atum, Amun, and Ra (who were sometimes considered the same god) and other gods involved with creation. Chapter six will unlock the deities of Duat, the underworld. Who were the other primary gods? What were their characteristics and roles? Which of the lesser gods stood out? Let's dig in and find out.

Osiris

We'll start with the children of the earth god Geb and the sky goddess Nut: Osiris, Isis, Set (Seth), Nephthys, and Horus the Elder. Who was Osiris? He eventually became the lord of the underworld and judge of the dead, but he didn't start out that way. We'll unpack the story of how he got there in the next chapter. Another name for this handsome god was *Wennefer*, or "Beautiful One." He was initially the "Lord of Love," a fertility god. One of his chief days of worship was when the Egyptians planted their crops after the Nile flooded its banks and left the land wet and fertile. Sowing the seeds represented fertility and the new life from the "dead" seed.

Osiris was the brother and husband of Isis. And yes, while it wasn't a custom among regular folks, the Egyptian royalty married their siblings. It was all about keeping the royal blood in the family. Usually, the crown prince married one of his half-sisters, but sometimes it was a full sister.

The Egyptians apparently assumed their gods did the same thing, as many gods in their mythology married their sisters.

Osiris wasn't actually his Egyptian name—that's what the Romans called him. His Egyptian name was Usir, and it means "strong and commanding." His mother, Nut, had five children on five consecutive days, and he was born on the first day. Some scholars think that Osiris was not originally an Egyptian god but a Canaanite or Syrian deity, mainly because he was a shepherd god connected with the Nile Delta region in northern Egypt.

Banebdjedet, Osiris's soul, flanked by two snakes and two monkeys[15]

Canaan (today's Israel and Palestine) and Syria were known for their roaming herders. Egypt's lush delta was where the Nile divided into multiple tributaries before flowing into the Mediterranean Sea. Many folks from Syria and Canaan settled in the delta, beginning in the Middle Kingdom, which impacted Egyptian culture.

Osiris carried a shepherd's crook. Moreover, an aspect of Osiris's soul, his *ba*, was named Banebdjedet, and he had four ram heads. In the Nile Delta city of Mendes, the Egyptians worshiped a ram they considered an incarnation of Banebdjedet. When the ram died, they mummified and buried him in a sacred tomb.

Isis

Isis, the goddess of fertility and motherhood, was probably ancient Egypt's most beloved deity. They admired her for her loyalty to her husband, her selflessness, and her giving nature. She protected those who called on her and was a model mother. Even Rome embraced the worship of the mother goddess Isis after Egypt became part of the

Roman Empire. Her husband-brother was Osiris, and her son was Horus.

Isis with Pharoah Haremhab[16]

Like Osiris, her worship seemed to begin in the Nile Delta area, but soon, almost all Egyptians adored her. The Egyptians thought their kings were an incarnation of the god Horus. Since Horus was the son of Osiris and Isis, they believed Isis was, in a sense, the mother of all the pharaohs. One of her titles was "Queen of the Throne." Her symbols include a scorpion (her protector), a sistrum (something like a rattle), and a falcon (which she shape-shifted into).

The Egyptians called Isis the "Enchantress" or "Lady of Words of Power." The Egyptians believed her words were so powerful that she could destroy life or create it. She was among several Egyptian deities who caused the annual flooding of the Nile. This crucial event allowed the Egyptians to grow enough food to feed everyone with enough left over to sell to other nations.

Set (Seth)

Set, or Seth, the brother of Osiris, Isis, and Horus the Elder, was probably the least favorite god of the ancient Egyptians. We'll find out why in the next chapter covering the Osiris myth. Aside from his grisly role in the myth, he was the god of chaos, storms, and war. His name meant "destroyer." As the opposite of Maat, Set was the bad guy who went about sowing disorder and instigating confusion.

His wife was his sister Nephthys, and their son was the wolf-headed Wepwawet. The Egyptians usually portrayed Set as a man with an aardvark head. How he and Nephthys (who had an ordinary woman's head) had a son with a canine head is a mystery.

Set was originally the god of "Upper Egypt" (Egypt's southern highlands) and the desert. He

Set (Seth), god of storms and chaos[17]

wasn't all bad. Lovestruck young Egyptians called on his magic to win the person of their dreams. He also helped Ra in his underworld struggle against the serpent Apep. Set was a popular god with the Hyksos, a people probably from Syria or Lebanon who ruled Egypt between the

Middle Kingdom and the New Kingdom. They thought he was the Egyptian version of their favorite god, Baal. The Egyptians found it appalling that the Hyksos king Apepi worshiped Set over the other Egyptian gods.

Nephthys

This goddess, also known as Nebet-het, was the sister of Osiris, Isis, and Horus the Elder and the sister-wife of Set. Nephthys was a goddess of beer but also of death, embalming, mourning, and decay. Like her sister, Isis, she protected mummies and the souls of the dead. Thus, the Egyptians were sure to give the "Friend of the Dead" proper reverence with professional mourners when a loved one died. Nephthys also protected the reigning pharaoh, spewing out fire on anyone who threatened him. Demons trembled in her presence.

Nephthys[18]

The Egyptians often pictured Nephthys as a kite (something like a hawk). Her relationship with her husband, Set, was complicated. Sometimes, she helped him in his evil schemes but then turned around and tried to undo them. Nephthys encouraged Set's good actions, like fighting the snake Apep so that Ra could make it through the underworld. She was close to her sister, Isis, and helped nurse her son, Horus.

Horus the Elder

Egyptian mythology identified two renowned gods named Horus, both of whom were portrayed as falcons and gods of the sky. Horus the Elder was the youngest son of Geb and Nut. Many myths say Horus was their grandchild, not their son, but it makes the myth about the five extra days of the year work out. Thus, some scholars insist there were two gods named Horus. Horus the Elder was the brother of Osiris, Isis, Set, and Nephthys. His Egyptian title was *Harwer*, which meant "Horus the Great."

In one myth, his wife is Hathor, the Eye of Ra, who almost wiped out humanity. Some myths equate him with Ra, sailing his solar barque across the sky. Other myths said Ra became Horus when he emerged from the underworld. Yet another myth says that one of Horus's eyes is the sun, and the other is the moon. Remember that these myths emerged in various parts of Egypt; hence, there were assorted, sometimes conflicting ideas about him. His worship extended back to Predynastic Egypt (before 3100 BCE) when the kings called themselves "Followers of Horus." Early carvings of kings show a falcon near them, representing Horus.

King Narmer with Horus, the Elder, as a falcon next to him, circa 3100 BCE[19]

The Other Horus

Osiris and Isis named their son Horus, so Horus the Elder was his uncle. However, the two Horuses had such similar characteristics that some scholars think they were the same god. Horus the Elder was important in Egypt's earlier history. Later, the younger Horus became famous, and everyone forgot about his uncle. This younger Horus remained a chief god of the Egyptians until Egypt fell to Rome in 30 BCE. The Greeks adopted this god and called him Harpocrates, and the Romans worshiped him and his mother, Isis.

Horus was conceived in unusual circumstances and had to fight his uncle Set to restore order in Egypt. We'll dig into that story in the next chapter. However, once he triumphed over evil, the Egyptians called him *Horu-Sema-Tawy*, "Horus, Who Unites the Two Lands." Throughout various points of Egypt's history, the country was divided between Upper Egypt in the south and Lower Egypt, or the Nile Delta region in the north, near the Mediterranean Sea. Whenever a king managed to bring both Upper and Lower Egypt under one rule, the Egyptians applauded him as their champion. To the Egyptians, Horus was the uniter of Egypt and the one who brought and maintained Maat, and their pharaoh was the human representation of Horus.

The Egyptians also believed Horus was the sky (apparently replacing his grandmother, Nut, who had been exiled to the highest heavens). In some artwork, Horus is a little boy with his finger in his mouth, sitting on a lotus flower with his mother, Isis. He was also important in the underworld as the god who introduced the souls of the dead to his father, Osiris.

Horus guides a dead person into Duat.[20]

Bastet (and Sekhmet)

The ancient Egyptians deeply cherished their pet cats and treated them like royalty. They draped their cats in jewels and let them eat off their own plates. Their cats were their "protectors" because they killed deadly snakes and scorpions while keeping mice out of the grain. When a cat died, the Egyptians went into deep mourning and shaved their eyebrows. The mourning period lasted until their eyebrows grew back. They would have the cat mummified and buried in their own tombs. Others left their cat mummy in the temple of the cat-goddess Bastet. When the temple got too full of cat mummies, the priests buried them in a nearby trench.

Who was Bastet? She was initially a lioness-headed goddess of war. As a lioness, she was either the same as or the sister of the goddess Sekhmet, as both were daughters of Ra. Later, Bastet evolved into a domestic cat. Bastet was a vigilant protector of children, and the Egyptians considered her a goddess of the home and fertility. She was usually portrayed as a domestic cat or with a woman's body and a cat's head. Because of the Egyptian's reverence for Bastet and cats in general, killing a cat brought the death penalty. Bastet's annual festival involved sacrifices of wine, beer, fruit, and meat. Everyone then danced, sang to lively music, and passed around the beer and wine.

Unfortunately, the Egyptians' reverence for Bastet was once used against them. When the Persian king Cambyses invaded Egypt in 525 BCE, the Egyptians held him off at first. But Cambyses had a military advisor named Phanes, who was Greek but had served in the Egyptian military as a paid mercenary. Phanes had gotten angry with the Egyptian pharaoh, left Egypt, and offered his services to the Persians. He suggested a crazy tactic to Cambyses. Knowing how fond the Egyptians were of cats and their reverence for Bastet, he recommended that the Persians paint Bastet's image on their shields. Then, the Persians released dozens of cats on their front lines and other sacred Egyptian animals, like rams, ibises, and dogs.

Bastet, the cat-headed goddess[11]

When the Egyptians saw a row of shields with Bastet on them, they paled. How could they shoot missiles at their goddess? And what about all those cats and other creatures roaming about? If they killed a sacred animal, the gods would be furious with them! They didn't dare fight the Persians, so they turned and fled. The Persians chased after them, killed 50,000 Egyptians, and made Egypt part of the Persian Empire.

34

Thoth was the baboon god of wisdom and writing.[22]

Thoth

Thoth was another favorite god of the Egyptians. He was the one who enabled Nut to give birth by winning moonlight from the moon god, Khonsu. Egyptian mythology says he created himself. He was among the earliest gods and married to Maat, goddess of order. Thoth was the god of justice, magic, order, and wisdom. He advised the other gods, especially when they had a dispute, and acted as their scribe. He created language and taught hieroglyphic writing to the Egyptians. While we might not think of monkeys as especially wise, the Egyptians portrayed Thoth as a baboon. Other times, he appears as a man with the head of an Ibis bird.

Taweret

The Egyptians had an unlikely goddess of children and pregnant women. Her name was Taweret, and she was part hippo, part crocodile, and part lioness. One of her titles was "Lady of the Birth House." While we might think of hippos as clumsy and amusing, the Egyptians were all too familiar with how dangerous they could be when protecting their young. Apparently, that's why they chose a partial hippopotamus goddess to guard children and help ladies in childbirth.

Hapi

Hapi wasn't the god of the Nile itself but of the Nile flooding. Egypt would be a barren wasteland if the Nile River did not flood every year from July to November. The part of Egypt along the Mediterranean coast gets a little rain, but the rest of Egypt receives almost none.

Taweret, goddess of childbirth and children[23]

Every year, heavy rainfall in the Ethiopian Highlands turned the Blue Nile into a swollen force that pushed into Egypt. The water flooded over its banks, immersing the surrounding land in nutrient-rich black silt. The Egyptians built dams around their fields with channels leading down to the Nile. The floodwaters turned the fields into lakes, saturating and enriching the soil. Once the flooding ended and the water receded, the farmers planted their crops in the soggy, rich soil. As long as the Nile flooded each year, the Egyptians had plenty to eat.

Hapi, god of the Nile flood[24]

The Egyptians believed that the god Hapi was responsible for this annual blessing. When the floods came, they said, "Hapi has arrived!" If the Nile didn't flood as it usually did, they thought they had done something to offend Hapi. Egypt had many weird-looking gods, but Hapi was unusual because he had male and female characteristics. He had a woman's breasts and a swollen belly like a pregnant woman. These represented the fertility he brought to Egypt. He had a beard and blue skin, representing water.

Sobek

Sobek was the Egyptian crocodile god of the military and male fertility. Like the Nile crocodile, he was aggressive and vicious. He was worshiped by Sobekneferu, Egypt's first woman pharaoh (the first who did not act as a regent for her son). The Egyptians began worshiping Sobek by at least the Old Kingdom and continued for 3,000 years into the Roman Empire. His mother was Neith, who was worshiped in the western Nile Delta and Libya from ancient times as the creator of the universe and everything in it. Sobek was also worshiped in the Faiyum Lake region southwest of Cairo. Sobek fused with Horus or Ra in the Middle Kingdom, so he traveled through the sky like the sun. The Egyptians kept a live crocodile in his temple in Faiyum and mummified it when he died. Archaeologists have found cemeteries full of mummified crocodiles.

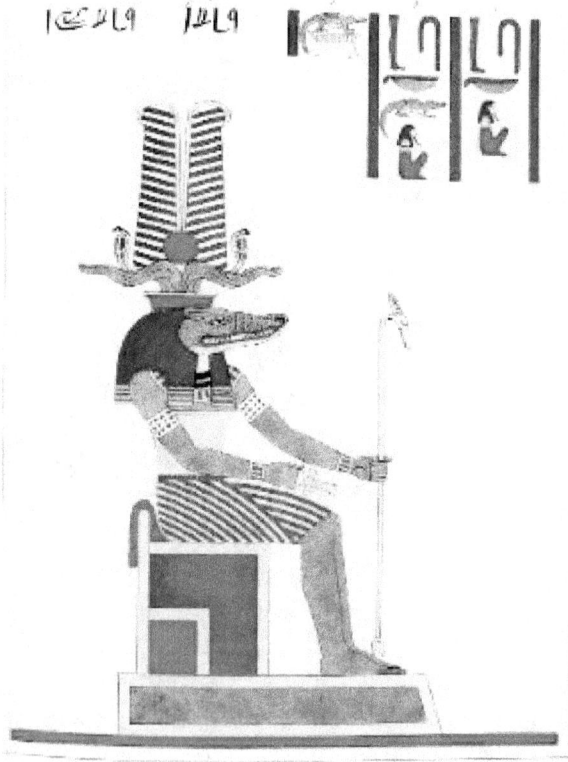

Sobek, the crocodile god[35]

Chapter 3 Activity

Check your answers in the back of the book.

1. I became the god of Duat, the underworld.
2. I was considered the mother of all pharaohs.
3. I was the destructive god of chaos and storms.
4. I was Set's wife and the "Friend of the Dead."
5. I was the sky god, son of Osiris and Isis.
6. I was a cat-headed goddess.
7. I was Maat's husband and god of wisdom.
8. I was the god of the Nile flood.
9. I was the crocodile god of the military.

A. Bastet
B. Hapi
C. Horus
D. Isis
E. Nephthys
F. Osiris
G. Set (Seth)
H. Sobek
I. Thoth

Chapter 4: The Osiris Myth

The Osiris myth was the most popular and enduring in ancient Egyptian mythology. It tells the story of a great battle between chaos and order in the cosmos. The myth contains hints of the biblical Cain and Abel, where one brother murdered the other in the early days of the world. Yet, the Osiris myth is also a story of resurrection and renewal of life. Its heroine is the relentless and resilient Isis, fiercely determined to undo evil.

How Old Is the Myth? What Are Its Sources?

The Osiris myth stretches back to at least the Old Kingdom. It may be loosely based on real-life struggles in Egypt's Predynastic era (4300-3100 BCE). The first known mention of the story appears around 2400 BCE in the Pyramid Texts. However, these inscriptions inside the pyramids simply alluded to the story, as if the scribes expected everyone to know it. The Shabaka Stone, a monument in the language of the Old Kingdom, refers to part of the Osiris myth. It says Osiris was buried in Memphis after he floated in from the sea. It also tells how Horus initially ruled Lower Egypt while Set ruled Upper Egypt, but Horus eventually united all of Egypt.

Parts of the story appear in the Middle Kingdom Coffin Texts and the New Kingdom Book of the Dead. The New Kingdom's "Great Hymn to Osiris" outlines the entire story but leaves out the details. A papyrus from Thebes dating to around 1140 BCE contains "The Contendings of Horus and Seth." Intriguingly, the first-century CE

Greek historian Plutarch gave the most complete account of the story using Egyptian texts that are now lost. He may have inserted elements of Greek mythology into the story.

Why Did Set Hate His Brother Osiris?

The Osiris myth begins with Osiris as "Lord of the Earth," meaning Egypt. His queen was his sister Isis. At that time, the Egyptians were not yet civilized. Osiris gave laws to his people and taught them how to farm, worship, sing, and play music. Under his kind and wise guidance, they learned how to live orderly lives in a society where everyone was equal. There was plenty of food and abundance in all things. No one needed weapons because peace was everywhere.

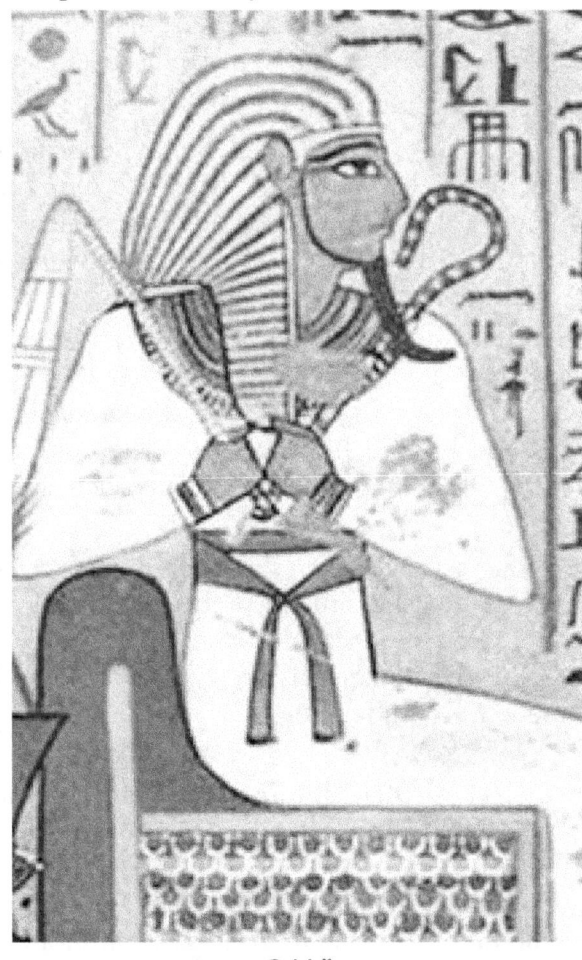

Osiris[26]

The myth isn't clear on why Set hated Osiris. He may have been jealous of his brother's power. The Pyramid Texts say that Osiris kicked Set, leaving his younger brother in a murderous rage. One version of the myth says that Set's wife, Nephthys, disguised herself as her sister Isis. It wasn't hard to do since they were twin sisters. Osiris slept with Nephthys, thinking she was his wife Isis, and she got pregnant.

Osiris's Murder and Isis's Search

In Plutarch's version, Set gathered seventy-two co-conspirators and joined forces with the Ethiopian queen Aso. They invited Osiris to join them in celebrating a festival. Osiris came, oblivious to their treachery. Before the party, Set built an exquisite ornamental chest that exactly matched Osiris's height and width. When the beautiful chest was brought into the party, the guests gathered around it admiringly.

"Whoever perfectly fits in this chest can have it!" Set promised.

The guests lay down in the chest one by one, but it didn't fit anyone. Finally, Osiris lay down in the chest, which fit him perfectly. The conspirators ran forward, slammed the lid, and nailed it shut. They hauled the chest down to the banks of the Nile and tossed it in the river, where it floated out to sea.

When Osiris didn't come home, Isis frantically searched everywhere for her husband. She asked everyone she met if they had seen him. Finally, some children told her how Set's friends had launched the chest into the river. Isis also learned how her sister, Nephthys, had betrayed her by sleeping with Osiris. Nephthys had abandoned the baby because she was afraid of Set.

Rather than getting revenge on her sister, Isis paused her search for Osiris, focusing on finding her infant nephew before he died. Finally, with the help of her dogs, she located the child. She named him Anubis and raised him in her home. Anubis grew up to become her guardian and right-hand man. After finding the baby, Isis resumed her search for Osiris.

Meanwhile, the chest that imprisoned Osiris floated into the Mediterranean Sea and up the coast to Lebanon. It got stuck in the branches of a tamarisk tree near the city of Byblos. The tree grew around the chest, encasing it with the body of Osiris inside. And yes—Egyptian gods could die. They weren't necessarily immortal.

One day, King Malcander of Byblos was strolling along the beach with his wife, Astarte. They walked around the tree, admiring its shape and beauty. The king had the tree cut down and installed as a decorative pillar in his palace. He had no idea that Osiris's body was trapped inside. Meanwhile, Isis had not given up the search for her husband. Through divine guidance, she arrived in Byblos.

Isis sat by a well disguised as an old woman. The queen's maidservants came to draw water and were friendly with her. Isis brightened up and braided their hair for them. As she did, fragrance wafted from her divine body. When the maids returned to the palace, they showed the queen their new hairstyles and told her of the lovely scent surrounding the older woman. The queen invited Isis to the palace and made her the nanny for her son. Once inside the palace, Isis quickly discerned that Osiris was inside the wooden pillar decorating the main hall.

As it turned out, goddesses aren't the best caregivers for mortal children. Isis loved the queen's baby and wanted him to be immortal. So, she initiated a magic ritual. The queen walked in to find her baby on fire. His nanny had shape-shifted into a swallow, flying around the rafters. Queen Astarte screamed and put out the fire, depriving the boy of immortality but saving his mortal life.

At this point, Isis revealed her true identity to the queen. "May I have that wooden pillar over there?"

Queen Astarte sputtered, "Yes! Yes! Take it! But please, leave immediately!"

Isis pulled the pillar down. She cut through the tree until she got to the chest and carried her husband's coffin away. When she was finally alone, Isis opened it and laid her face on the face of her dead husband, wailing in sorrow. Finally, she got up and sailed back to Egypt with the coffin. Arriving in Egypt, Isis hid her husband's body in the swampland of the Nile Delta.

Isis asked her sister Nephthys to guard the body while she searched for special herbs. Isis planned to make a magic brew to resurrect Osiris. However, Set had gone out hunting boars and came across the chest with Osiris inside. Nephthys was helpless to stop her enraged husband as he cut his brother's body into fourteen pieces and scattered them throughout the swamps and streams of the delta.

Resurrection and Birth

When Isis returned with the herbs, Nephthys told her what Set had done. The news was almost unbearable, but Isis was determined to save Osiris. "I'll go find him and put him back together!" she cried. "He will live again!"

Isis sailed through the rivers and bogs of the Nile Delta, looking for her husband's body parts. Nephthys and Thoth, the god of wisdom, helped her. After collecting the pieces of his body, she put him back together. Isis tightly wrapped strips of cloth around his body to hold everything in place, making Osiris the first mummy. Using the herbs she had collected, Isis made a potion and brought Osiris back to life, but only briefly. She flew around her husband in the form of a falcon and became pregnant. Sadly, she couldn't keep Osiris alive for long. He died again and became the king of Duat. We'll pick up his story in the underworld in chapter six.

Isis and baby Horus[27]

Isis and Horus Hide From Set

Isis grieved for Osiris, but her one consolation was that she carried his child. "Osiris will live on through my son!" Isis hid from Set in a thick patch of papyrus in the Nile Delta, waiting for her baby's birth. When he was born, she named him Horus but kept him hidden until he grew up.

In the years that Set ruled Egypt, the land dissolved into disorder and chaos. The wealth brought by Osiris melted away.

Horus's father, Osiris, appeared to him from time to time. He taught Horus wisdom and trained him as a warrior so he could retake Egypt from Set and restore order.

One day, Osiris asked Horus, "What's the most noble thing a person can do?"

"Avenge the evil done to his mother and father!" Horus replied.

Osiris smiled. "And what animal is the most useful in battle?"

"A horse!" Horus said.

"Really? Not a lion?" Osiris asked.

"Yes, a horse can race after the enemy and trample them!"

Osiris nodded. "You are ready and well prepared for your quest."

Horus with a falcon head[28]

The Contendings of Horus and Set

When Horus first confronted Set, he paled. Horus looked so much like Osiris. Could Horus be his son? Impossible! Set laughed. "You're no son of Osiris. I chopped him into pieces! You're some illegitimate child of my sister Isis."

Horus faced many battles with Set in a war to win back Egypt. "The Contendings of Horus and Seth" said neither god could prevail over the other. Horus and Isis appealed to the Ennead, the high court of the oldest gods. Horus told them how his uncle murdered his father and stole his kingdom.

Shu, the god of the atmosphere and grandfather of Osiris, Isis, and Set, was the first to weigh in: "Set has great power, yet young Horus has a just cause. We should grant justice to Horus and give him father's throne!"

Thoth, the god of wisdom, agreed. "This is a million times right!"

Hearing this, Isis cried out in joy. "North Wind, go whisper this news to Osiris."

Lord Shu proclaimed, "Thoth, give the royal signet ring to Horus. We will crown him Egypt's king!"

But Set wasn't ready to give up so easily. "Don't forget—I'm the one who slays Apep, the enemy of Ra, every night! I stand on the prow of the Boat of a Million Years. If not for me, the sun wouldn't rise in the morning. I should be the one on the throne of Osiris!"

The gods shuddered at the thought of Apep, the terrible Serpent of Chaos. "Set is right," they muttered.

Then, Horus the Elder, the brother of Osiris and Set, spoke up. "Is it right to give the throne to an uncle when the mortal son of the king is right here?"

But the creator, Atum-Ra, interjected, "Is it right to give the throne to a youngster whose mouth smells of his mother's breastmilk?"

Isis was furious with the Ennead's indecision. "The throne rightfully belongs to my son, Horus! Look at what happened in the past years when Set ruled Egypt. He has lost all the wealth my husband built up. Everything is in confusion and disorder. The humans will all die if Set keeps ruling!"

"She has a point. Egypt needs peace restored," the gods agreed. "All right. We pronounce justice for young Horus!"

Set turned red with fury. "How dare you! You cowards! I will get my great scepter. Each day, I'll strike one of you down with it! Furthermore, I refuse to argue my case if Isis is present in the court!"

Atum-Ra proclaimed, "In that case, we will cross the river to the island in the middle. We will try the case there. I forbid the ferryman to carry Isis across."

The gods crossed over, leaving Isis behind. But she was relentless in her quest for justice. Isis transformed herself into a hunchbacked old woman. The ferryman carried her over to the island in exchange for a golden ring.

The gods were enjoying a feast, yet Set sat apart from the rest. Isis abandoned her old woman disguise for that of a lovely young widow and approached Set.

Set perked up at the sight of the beautiful lady. "Who are you, pretty one? Why have you come here?"

Isis began weeping. "My great lord, I need a champion! My husband was a herdsman, and he died. So, my son cared for the cattle. But then a stranger arrived, took the cattle, and forced us out of our home! Oh, my lord, Please help us! Champion our cause!"

Set bristled in indignation and wiped Isis's tears from her face. "Please don't cry, lovely lady. I will be your defender! How dare this villain take your husband's property while your son is still alive?"

Isis shape-shifted into a kite and flew up into an acacia tree, shrieking in hysterical laughter. "Set, it's your turn to cry now! You just judged your own case. You condemned yourself!"

The other gods were drawn to the commotion. "What's going on?"

Set sputtered, "That cunning Isis has tricked me!"

Ra replied, "You have judged yourself, Set!"

Part of the Ennead[39]

The Ennead crossed back over the river, planning for Horus's coronation. Yet, Set refused to admit defeat. "Horus, I challenge you! Let's shape-shift into hippos and fight underwater in the river. Whoever comes to the surface first is the loser!"

Horus agreed. Isis collapsed to the ground, weeping, certain that Set would kill Horus. The two gods dove under the surface of the Nile, and the struggle raged for days. Finally, Isis could bear it no more. She made a magic harpoon and threw it into the churning water. Instead of hitting Set, it impaled Horus's hip. He broke the surface in a rage. "Mother! You punctured me with your spear!"

Isis used her magic to recall her harpoon and threw it a second time, piercing Set.

"Sister!" Set wailed. "Why do you always have to be my enemy? I'm your brother! Release me."

Isis felt sorry for her brother and let him go. This enraged Horus. He jumped out of the river, sliced his mother's head off with one stroke of his knife, and then stalked off to the Mountains of the West. The headless Isis walked toward the other horrified gods. Thoth had words of power and put Isis's head back on. Yet, now it was a cow's head.

Set followed after Horus and found him asleep under a palm tree. He grabbed his nephew and gouged his eyes out. He returned to the other gods and told them he couldn't find a sign of Horus anywhere. Yet, the goddess Hathor, the Eye of Ra, found Horus in agony. She dripped milk from a gazelle into his eye sockets, restored his eyes, and led him back to the Ennead.

"Set lied to you. He blinded Horus! I healed him, and here he is."

Ra summoned the two contenders, scolded them for their violence, and insisted they stop fighting.

"One more contest!" Set demanded. "We'll both build stone ships and race them down the Nile. The winner will wear Osiris's crown!"

Horus agreed, so Set sliced off the top of a mountain with his club. He built his massive ship from the stone and hauled it to the river. He was surprised to see Horus already there, floating in his boat. Horus had built his ship from pine but covered it with plaster, making it appear to be stone. When Set threw his stone ship into the Nile, it sank to the bottom as the gods roared in laughter. Set shape-shifted into a red hippopotamus again and attacked Horus's boat, sinking it.

When Horus tried to spear Set, the Ennead yelled at him to stop. Horus waded to shore and stood dripping before the Ennead in a fury. "It's now been eighty years I have contended with Set! You don't know how to judge us!"

Atum-Ra asked the other gods, "What do we do?"

How Did the Story End?

Atum-Ra's son, Geb, took matters into his own hands. He called Set and Horus before him.

"Set, you are the king of southern Egypt. Horus, you are the king of northern Egypt."

With one pronouncement, Geb divided Egypt. Each king marched away to his piece of Egypt. But Horus was not content with the ruling. "I should have *all* Egypt. I've been defrauded!"

Thoth and Shu sent a messenger with a letter to Osiris in the underworld. When the messenger returned, he brought Osiris's angry reply. "Why did you rob my son of my throne? Don't forget that I'm the Lord of Duat. I'll unleash my demons on the land of the living, and they will carve out your hearts!"

The gods trembled—even Atum-Ra, the creator.

Geb cleared his throat. "I am giving all of Egypt to Horus. He is the son of my firstborn He alone will rule all of Egypt!"

Amazingly, Horus and Set put their quarrels aside and made peace. King Horus brought Maat back to Egypt. Order and justice reigned again.

Chapter 4 Activity

Check the answers in the back of the book.

1. Who murdered Osiris?
   a. Geb   b. Set   c. Isis   d. Sobek

2. Where did Isis find her dead husband?
   a. Byblos   b. Heliopolis   c. Memphis   d. Thebes

3. How long did Set and Horus struggle over Egypt's throne?
   a. Five years   b. Fifteen years   c. Forty years   d. Eighty years

4. Who won the Battle of the Hippos?
   a. Horus   b. Set   c. Neither   d. The Ennead

5. Who finally decided who would rule Egypt?
   a. Atum-Ra   b. Geb   c. Isis   d. The Ennead

Chapter 5: Isis and the Scorpion Myths

Egypt is home to two deadly species of scorpions: the deathstalker and the Arabian fat-tailed scorpion. They prey on insects and small lizards but can be lethal to humans if someone inadvertently touches one and gets stung. Scorpions hide in dark nooks and crannies, so the jar a person reaches for might have a scorpion latched to the back. They could be lurking in stored clothing or even in a bed. These Egyptian scorpions are among the most dangerous in the world. The venom of both species has neurotoxins and cardiotoxins, so their sting can cause heart attacks, internal bleeding, and difficulty breathing.

Naturally, the ancient Egyptians had a healthy fear of scorpions. They were terrified that one might sting a baby or small child, who would be more susceptible to the poison. They had magic spells to pronounce over someone stung by a scorpion to break the power of the poison. Their incantations included cursing the venom as if it were a demon.

They also had medical treatment. If someone had a scorpion sting or snakebite, a doctor cut the wound and sucked out the poison. These priest-doctors inscribed some of these treatments and magic spells on a stone monument called the "Horus on the Crocodiles Stela."

Horus on the Crocodiles Stela

The Horus on the Crocodiles Stela (also called the Metternich Stela) stood in Heliopolis and later Alexandria, Egypt, for over 2,000 years. On the front of the stela is an image of Horus as a toddler, standing on two crocodiles. His hands clutch scorpions, snakes, an antelope, and a lion. The ibis-headed god Thoth stands on his left, and Ra and Isis are on his right. They are all balancing on coiled snakes. The stela (or stele) had thirteen incantations against snakebites, scorpion stings, or other poisons. The victim or priest was supposed to recite the spells to rid the venom from the person's body. A priest poured water over the stone, caught it at the bottom, and gave it to the victim to drink.

The Horus on the Crocodiles Stela[80]

At the base of the stela is an inscription in which Isis relates the cure used by Thoth when a scorpion stung little Horus. It happened when Isis and Horus were hiding out in the marshland from Set. Set vowed to kill the child and sent a scorpion to sting Horus. Isis had left Horus to beg for food, and she returned to a horrifying sight. Tears covered

Horus's face, and foam came out of his mouth. He was limp, but Isis detected a faint heartbeat.

Isis screamed to her child, "Wake up! I'm here!"

Yet, he didn't respond. Isis put him to her breast to nurse, but he was too weak. Fear consumed Isis. Who could she call for help? Her oldest brother (and husband) was dead. Her brother, Set, was her enemy, and her sister, Nephthys, was his wife. She had to call on the humans. As she screamed out, the people of the Nile Delta came to her aid. They tried babbling this spell and that, but none of their incantations could cure the baby. The people wept with Isis, sure that the baby was doomed.

Finally, a noblewoman from the village spoke to the mother and her child. "Don't fear, Horus! Don't despair, mother. Set cannot harm the boy here. Atum-Ra, father of the gods, will help you. Try to figure out what happened to the baby. Maybe a scorpion stung him, or a snake bit him. Don't be afraid. Horus will live!"

Isis put her nose in the baby's mouth and smelt death. She realized a scorpion sting had poisoned him. She scooped him up and began jumping around, wailing in grief and calling out to Ra for help.

"Oh, Ra, Horus has been stung! My helpless, fatherless child, my innocent one! He was destined to avenge his father!"

Ra was floating through the sky in his Boat of a Million Years when Isis called out. He stopped the sun in the middle of the sky. Thoth, the god of wisdom, was with him on the boat, so Ra sent him down to Earth to help Isis. Thoth chanted a series of incantations over the little boy.

"Awake, Horus! Poison, retreat! Ra's mouth curses you. Come out on the ground, poison! May hearts rejoice and light pervade. The poison is powerless. Flow out, poison! You are weak and have lost your strength. Horus has defeated the enemy."

The little boy recovered and grew up to fulfill his destiny. The inscriptions on the stela imply that other people could call out these spells against an array of afflictions, and they would be healed.

Other spells on the stela included one against the scary serpent Apep, who waged war against Ra in the underworld each night. When a person chanted the incantation, Apep's head flew off, and his body caught fire and burned to ashes. Another spell caused Apep to vomit. The priests used this incantation for someone who ate or drank poison. When they spoke the magic words, the person vomited out the poison.

A third spell was for a cat stung by a scorpion, asking Ra to help the cat in her quest to get rid of the poison. "Oh, Ra, come to your daughter! A scorpion has stung her, and the poison has entered her body and is spreading throughout her body. Come in your power and wrath!"

The incantation continued, with Ra naming body parts affected by the poison and naming a deity who would help in that area. Isis and Nephthys are called up at the end of the spell to weave in their healing protection. The priests used this spell not only for cats but also for people.

Isis-Serket, the Scorpion Goddess[81]

Isis as Serket, the Scorpion Goddess and Patron of Doctors

Although a scorpion nearly killed her child, Isis sometimes took on the form of Iset Ta-Wahaet, or Isis, the Scorpion Goddess. She merged with the goddess Serket, whose name meant "she who causes the throat to breathe." This name alluded to Serket's healing powers from scorpion venom. (The neurotoxin in venom causes the throat to swell, so the victim chokes to death.) When women ritually wept at Isis's temple at Gebtu in southern Egypt, they could supposedly walk through scorpions without being stung.

The male and female priests of Isis-Serket were also doctors called the "Followers of Serket." Isis-Serket was the patron of these doctors, and the physicians frequently called on her name for healing. The "Rites of Serket" were chants and magic spells intended to drive out disease and poisons and bring health and well-being. These priests spoke of the "House of Life," which wasn't a physical building but the promise of healing. It was something that Serket's priests and priestesses carried within them in their knowledge of the healing arts and magic.

In ancient Egypt, doctoring was a blend of scientific method and magic. The priest-doctors carefully observed their patients, checking their pulse and asking about their symptoms. They consulted medical texts to help diagnose and treat the problem. (The Egyptian medical texts were a vast collection telling how to diagnose and treat injuries and diseases.) The priest would also consider whether he or she had enough skill to heal the patient. It required medical knowledge, an understanding of which spells to use, and the power to exorcise the demons causing disease.

The Seven Scorpions

Another story on the "Horus on the Crocodiles Stela" was "Isis and the Seven Scorpions." To avoid attracting Set's attention, Issi disguised herself as an older woman. Thoth assigned seven gigantic scorpions to guard her. Three scorpions, named Petet, Matet, and Thetet, walked ahead of her, scanning the region for danger. Mestet protected Isis on her right side and Mestetef on her left. Tefen and Befen provided the rear guard.

Thoth sent seven scorpions to protect Isis and Horus.[32]

Of course, trying to blend into her surroundings didn't work well when encircled by giant scorpions. Isis sternly warned the scorpions, "Don't you dare look at any children or other helpless creatures! Leave them alone! Your job is to protect Horus and me from danger."

Isis needed food for Horus and herself, so she walked to the city of Per-sui, bordering the marshland. Her walk had been long and hot, and Isis was tired and hungry. She saw a large house in front of her with a woman named Usert, a leader in the town, standing at the door. Isis walked toward the house, but Usert began trembling when she saw the scorpions. She jumped inside and slammed the door.

"Well! That was rude," muttered the scorpions.

Isis was crestfallen when Usert closed the door in her face, but she could understand why. After all, she had almost lost Horus to a scorpion sting. Isis continued walking down the street with the scorpions until they came to the modest cottage of an elderly, impoverished woman. She told the woman she needed food for herself and her child.

"Come in! Come in!" the old lady politely greeted her. "You must be tired and thirsty. Here, sit down and rest! Drink some water. I'll pack some food for you and your child."

While Isis was resting in the poor woman's cottage, her scorpion bodyguard was holding a council of war. "We can't let Usert get away with this outrage. How dare she reject the goddess! We should get revenge!"

All the scorpions agreed that Usert must be punished. The scorpion Tefen told the other six, "Quickly, everyone! Put your poison on my tail. I'll carry it to Usert's home."

So, the other scorpions put their poison on Tefen's tail, making his sting six times more deadly. He scuttled back to Usert's house and slithered under the closed door. Tefen swiftly scurried over to Usert's little son and stung him. No sooner had he harmed the boy than flames filled the house, signaling the gods' anger. The heavens opened, and rain poured down on Usert's house, even though it was the dry season.

Usert was beside herself. The boy was dying. What could she do? She grabbed him up and carried his limp body outside into the street, screaming for help. Everyone rushed out of their houses at her wailing, but no one knew what to do to save the boy. As she ran through the streets, desperately shrieking, Isis heard the uproar and stepped out of the old lady's cottage. The goddess took pity on Usert and her little boy.

She had experienced the same thing and knew the utter helplessness the mother was feeling.

Isis scolded the scorpions. "Didn't I tell you to leave children alone? I told you not to even look at them! Now, see what you've done! This is an innocent child. Your job is to protect me, not kill children!"

The scorpions slunk into the shadows, ashamed. Isis turned to Usert and her child in compassion. Her heart was troubled. How could she save the life of this innocent one?

She called to Usert, "Come here! I can help you. Life is in my mouth. I'm famous in my hometown for driving reptiles away with my incantations. My father taught me how to do this, and I am his beloved daughter."

A statue of Isis in King Tut's tomb[33]

Trembling, Usert brought the boy to Isis, who massaged the child's throat. As she did, Isis chanted her magic over the boy. "Poison of Tefen, come out now! Drip to the ground. Don't penetrate the child. Don't enter his body."

Isis continued chanting as she embraced the child's cold body. "My voice can awaken the dead. I will now call out my words of power. I will bring life back to the lifeless."

Isis spoke to the poison from the other six scorpions, one by one, commanding their venom to leave the boy. "I am the goddess Isis! I am the Lady of Magic! My words are glorious and magical. Every creature that stings bows to me. My father, Geb, gave me his magic to drive out poison. So, now, vile poison, you are powerless! Retreat now! Leave this innocent one. Poison die! Child, live! By the power of Ra, the poison dies. As Horus was cured of the scorpion sting, this child will likewise rise fully healed!"

Isis made a poultice of bread and spelt (an ancient type of wheat) and applied it to the spot where Tefen had stung him. It pulled the poison out of the boy's body, and he recovered. At that moment, the fire in Usert's home went out, and the rain stopped falling. Usert collapsed to the ground, sobbing in relief. From that point on, the Egyptians made a poultice of salt and wheat flour and applied it to scorpion stings. They pronounced the words of power that Isis used to revive Usert's son.

Usert was pierced to the heart with shame that she had closed her door to Isis. She rushed home to gather her gold and silver neck ornaments and bracelets. She knelt at Isis's feet, placing her treasures before the goddess.

"I'm so ashamed. I turned you away from my home in your time of need, and yet you took pity on me in my distress and healed my son!"

Usert kissed Isis, then turned to the impoverished elderly woman who had welcomed Isis into her home.

"You are ten times better than me. You offered kindness and shelter to a stranger in need, although you did not know her."

Usert filled the old lady's home with jewels and other valuable items, enabling her to live comfortably for the rest of her days. After everything calmed down, it was time for Isis to return home to Horus. He was waiting in a nest of papyrus on the island of Chemmis in the Nile Delta.

As Isis walked out of the town, her scorpion escorts followed her. Isis wheeled and gave stern orders to the seven. "Keep your eyes on the road! Don't you dare lift your eyes until we get back to the swamp!"

The chastened scorpions bowed their heads. They quickly assumed their positions around the goddess as they walked through the marshland to the floating island of Chemmis.

Isis holding Horus[84]

Chapter 5 Activity

Choose the correct word(s) for each blank space from the list below. Check your answers in the back of the book.

The _____ had inscriptions and stories about treating scorpion stings and snakebites with magic and medicine. A carving of the little boy Horus on the monument showed him holding _____ in his hands. The monument tells the story of how wicked uncle _____ sent a scorpion to sting baby Horus. When Isis called out to ____ for help, he stopped the sun in the sky and sent _____ down to help. He chanted _____ to heal little Horus.

Isis merged with the goddess Serket to become the _____. Thoth assigned seven scorpions to _____ Isis from Set and other dangers. But the scorpions got mad at a woman who refused to help Isis. They disobeyed Isis and stung the woman's _____. Isis forgave the woman and took pity on her son. She used her magic to heal him. The woman was sorry for not inviting Isis into her home. She gave _____ to Isis and to the poor old woman in the village who had been kind to the goddess.

Horus on the Crocodiles Stela	incantations
protect	Ra
Scorpion Goddess	Set
scorpions, snakes, an antelope, and a lion	son
Thoth	treasure

Chapter 6: Tales from Duat (the Underworld)

The ancient Egyptians clearly believed in life after death, but what did they think it was like? They had elaborate ideas about Duat and the perilous journey there. Egyptian mythology explained who would get into the "Field of Reeds" and who wouldn't. What happened to the ones who didn't get in? This chapter will dig into that and the Egyptians' other ideas about the underworld.

The Human Soul: Ba and Ka

The ancient Egyptians believed the soul had two aspects. They believed that their *ka* was their true identity, their personality. It remained on Earth, generally in or near the person's dead body. The Egyptians left food and beer at the graves of a loved one so his or her soul could eat. The *ba* was the part of the soul that separated from the body when a person died. Like a flying bird, it traveled to Duat, struggled through all its perils, and hopefully made it to paradise, "The Field of Reeds."

The ka (and some believed the ba) returned to the dead person's tomb at night to rest. If a person wasn't properly mummified when they died, the soul could not return to a decomposing body. Another hazard was that they might get lost on the way back. In either case, the person's soul would stop existing.

Anubis, His Demons, and the Leopard's Spots

As mentioned earlier, Anubis was the son of Osiris from an extramarital affair with Nephthys who was raised by his aunt, Isis. The jackal-headed Anubis was a key player in everyone's death. He presided over their mummification and their judgment in the Hall of Truth. In fact, he was the original god of death in Egypt's earlier days until Osiris died and took on the role.

But Anubis was still a powerful force in the underworld, leading a horde of demons who guarded the portals of Duat. When entering Duat, newly dead people had to know the demons' names and rank. They also had to have followed the principles of Maat in their lifetime, extending harmony and justice to those around them. If they had lived unjust lives or failed to properly greet the demons, the dark spirits barred their way, extinguishing the person's soul.

The priest on the left wears a leopard skin, and the one on the right wears a jackal mask, representing Anubis as he holds up the mummy.[35]

In one myth, the evil god Set shapeshifted into a leopard to get to Osiris's body. In those days, leopards didn't have spots but a solid coat, like a lion. However, Anubis caught him in the act. He grabbed a hot iron to protect his father and started poking Set all over his body. The burned areas became the spots that leopards have now. Anubis skinned Set and wore his spotted leopard coat. In Egyptian burial rituals, one priest wore a jackal head like Anubis, and the high priest wore a leopard skin.

What Were Mummies All About?

The ancient Egyptians had to preserve the bodies of the dead so the soul would live on. The mummification process prevented decay. Dozens of Egyptian mummies have survived to modern days. They are remarkably preserved, considering they were mummified two or three millennia ago. Anubis presided over the mummification of a body, with a priest wearing a jackal head to represent him.

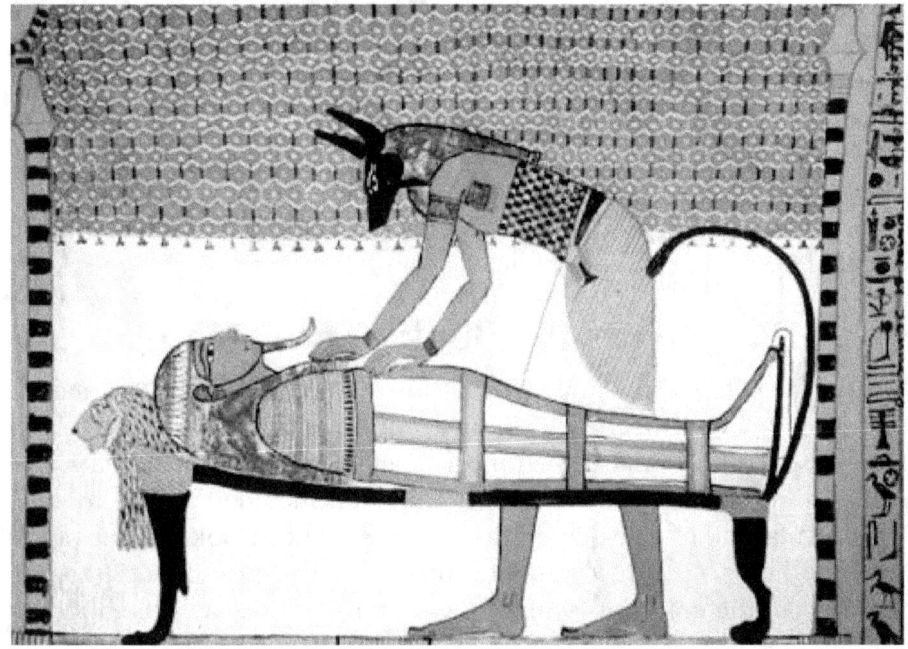

The priest of Anubis embalming a dead person[36]

The priests removed the person's body organs and dried them in jars of natron salt for seventy days. They also covered the body in natron to dry and preserve it. Then, they either put the dried organs back in the body or left them in jars that were buried with the mummy. After the body dried, they covered it with black resin to seal it and prevent fungal growth. Then, they encased the entire body in linen strips, forming the mummy.

Finally, they placed a decorative mask in the person's image over the face. The mummy went inside a wooden coffin. The coffin of a prestigious person was placed inside a giant stone box called a sarcophagus that was carved and painted to look like the dead person. The priests put the sarcophagus in a tomb with beer, food, games, furniture, and other things the person would need in the next life.

What Were "Westerners?" How Did People Prepare for Their Journey West?

The sun-god Ra descended into the underworld when the sun set in the west. Thus, ancient Egyptians believed Duat lay to the west. If a person died, they said he or she was going on a westward journey, so they called dead souls "Westerners." Anubis was called "The First of the Westerners" because of his pivotal role in people entering Duat.

To prepare for their journey west, the ancient Egyptians ensured they had certain things buried with them to guide their way and protect them. They collected writings from the Book of the Dead and wore amulets to protect their soul from demons. Speaking of demons, ancient Egyptians had to learn the names of the important ones who guarded the gates of Duat and how to greet them politely.

What Was the Book of the Dead?

The Book of the Dead was a collection of papyrus scrolls containing everything a person needed to know to make it from their tomb to the paradise section of Duat. It had magic spells and special instructions for dealing with demons and other perils. It even included a map to guide them through the gates and passageways. The Book of the Dead described how to conduct a funeral properly. The priests put a copy of the scrolls in the coffin or tomb of the deceased to use as a handbook in navigating Duat.

Multiple versions of the Book of the Dead were written over the millennia. They came with illustrations. One curious ghostlike figure among the hieroglyphics was Medjed. He had legs and feet projecting from his dome-shaped white body with huge eyes. The Book of the Dead called him the "unseen smiter who shoots with his eyes and sends fiery blasts from his mouth." Except, he doesn't appear to have a mouth!

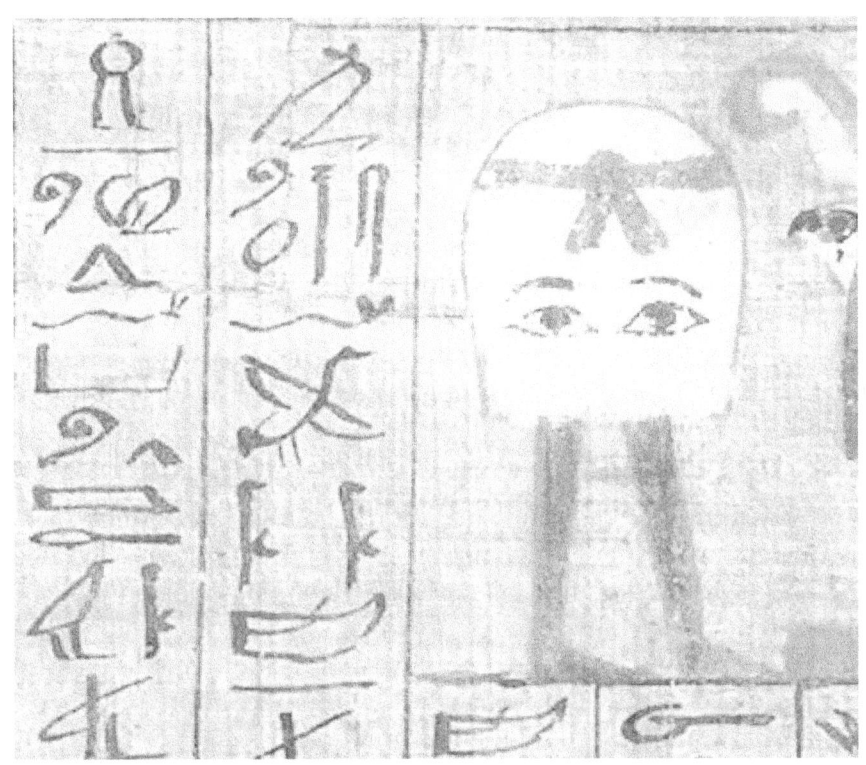
Medjed the Smiter in the Book of the Dead[87]

What Was the Journey through Duat Like?

When the soul left its body, it had to fight through the first three chambers of Duat on the way to the Hall of Truth. A monstrous fire-breathing serpent guarded each gate. Hence, a soul had to remember the correct magic to use or carry a copy of the Book of the Dead, which had all the necessary spells. The journey was dark and brutal. Some souls didn't make it and passed into oblivion.

The passage followed a great river called the Winding Waterway. Even the gods couldn't navigate this treacherous river filled with dangerous creatures. The soul had to hope it could persuade Hraf-Haf, the ferryman of the gods, to take it on his boat. Hraf-Haf had eyes in the back of his head and was half-human and half-crocodile.

After a pharaoh died, his sorcerers spent weeks chanting incantations to help his soul through Duat. Sometimes, they threatened Hraf-Haf with the wrath of the god Thoth if he failed to ferry the pharaoh.

Sassy Kings Who Stood Up to the Underworld's Gods and Monsters

Especially in the Old Kingdom, the Egyptian kings tried to terrorize the gods and monsters of Duat so they could pass smoothly through. They and their priests would chant these threats and inscribe them in their pyramids: "Watch out! I'm coming into your territory. I'm going to chop you up and eat you alive! I'll cook and eat your intestines! I'll crush your bones and suck the marrow out. I'll eat your heart." By munching on a minor god, a king could steal his superpowers.

A Cool Drink of Water at the Hall of Truth

Not all the gods and superhuman creatures in Duat were out to get the souls of humans. When souls finally made it through the three hellish chambers and arrived at the Hall of Truth, the kind goddess Qebhet met them with a cool drink of water. Qebhet was Anubis's daughter and appeared as an ostrich or snake holding water. She helped revive souls after their horrendous journey and offer them comfort. Qebhet also assisted souls in moving out of their mortal body.

What Was the Test to Get into Paradise?

When Anubis led a soul into the Hall of Truth, an array of gods awaited. Osiris sat on his throne as the god of the dead. Everyone who reached the Hall of Truth came before Osiris for judgment. Anubis moved to the center and knelt at some scales to weigh the person's heart. The gods of the Ennead sat on their thrones to judge the procedure. Behind Anubis was a creature called Ammit. She had a crocodile head, a hippopotamus's hindquarters, and a lion's forequarters. Thoth stood ready to record the results of the judgment.

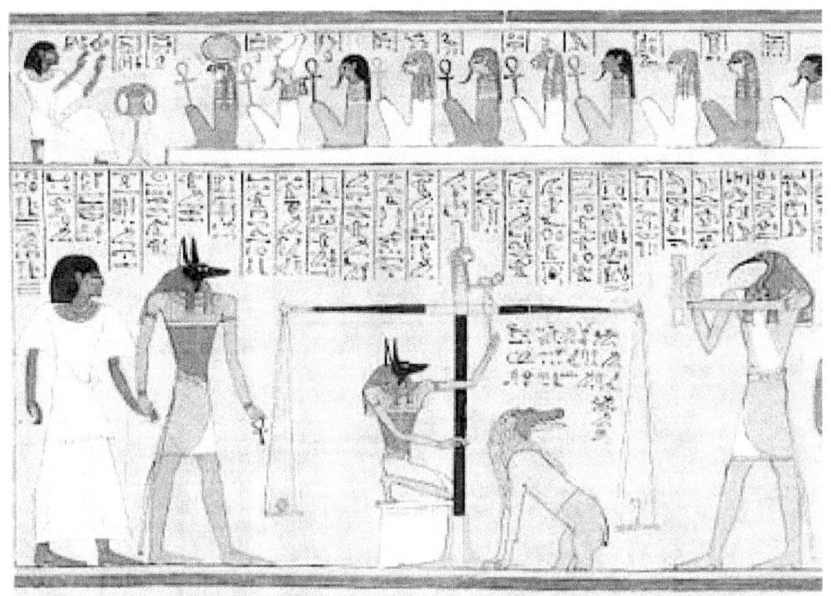

A man named Hunefer (far left) faces the scales of justice. The Ennead sits above.[38]

The first thing the soul facing judgment had to do was recite all the sins he or she had *not* committed. The person had to go through a list of forty-two sins and confirm his or her innocence. "I haven't made anyone cry. I haven't acted in rage. I have not killed anyone. I haven't lied. I haven't used swear words. I have not cheated on my wife/husband. I have not raised my voice."

Yes, the requirements for paradise were strict. They got even more stringent with part two of the judgment. It was time to weigh the heart in the balance against the feather of truth. On one side of the scale, Anubis placed a feather from the wing of Maat, the goddess of law and order. He put the heart of the person being judged on the other. If the person had lived a life of harmony, order, peace, and justice, their heart was as "light as a feather." It passed the test. However, a heart weighed down with conflict, chaos, violence, and injustice failed the test.

Horus introduced the souls that had passed to his father, Osiris, sitting on his throne. Isis and Nephthys stood behind the throne to welcome the new soul.

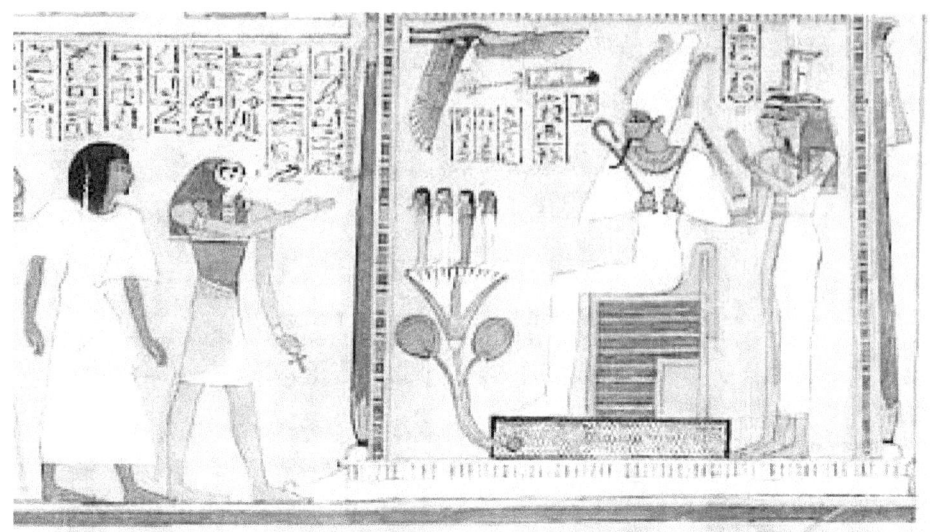

Hunefer passed! Horus introduces him to Osiris, Isis, and Nephthys.[39]

What Happened to People Who Failed the Test?

Which is worse—being eaten by a monster or thrown into the Lake of Fire? Egyptian mythology had two potential punishments for people whose hearts were too heavy with conflict and injustice. Both punishments ended in the destruction of the person, body and soul. He or she no longer existed in any form.

In one version of the myth, the crocodile-lion-hippo Ammit, "Devourer of the Dead," gobbled up anyone who failed the test. The Book of the Dead and the Coffin Texts describe a fiery lake in Duat, guarded by four baboons, where those found guilty died. In some versions of the myth, the monster Ammit ate the heart, and the rest of the person was thrown into the Lake of Fire.

What Was Auru Like?

The people who passed the test were non-violent and never cheated anyone. They were the people who helped widows, orphans, and shipwreck survivors. They gave food and clothing to the hungry and poor, never caused anyone to cry, and never stirred up arguments. Those who passed the test were carried in a boat over the Lily Lake to Aaru (the Field of Reeds), the Egyptian paradise.

Aaru was part of Duat. It wasn't up in the heavens somewhere; it was down below. Aaru was something like the Nile Delta. It had lush islands of reeds floating in rivers and lakes. Unlike the Nile Delta, it had trees of turquoise. A duplicate of a person's former home was there, along with the spirits of all their loved ones who had been mummified. If they had mummified their favorite cat or other pets, the animals would be waiting for them. The souls that made it to Aaru had plenty of food and beer to enjoy.

Aaru was a wonderful place for farming, fishing, and hunting. And yes, while fishing and hunting might sound like fun, farming is work! Many Egyptians weren't too excited about that part. They were ready to take a rest. But they had to grow food to eat, and how would that happen? They buried little dolls called *shabtis* in their grave. The Book of the Dead gave the proper spell to speak over them, making them come to life. The dolls could do all the hard farm labor while their owner rested. They were the workforce in paradise. Most folks tried to take as many shabtis with them as they could afford.

Shabti dolls[40]

A Prince and a Magician Visit to Duat

The Book of Thoth is a collection of writings supposedly written by Thoth, the god of wisdom. One of the stories in this collection is "The Land of Dead," a tale of two living people who make a trip to Duat. The legend takes place in the New Kingdom. It features Prince Setna (Khaemweset), the son of the famous pharaoh, Rameses II. Rameses had at least fifty sons, but Setna was his fourth. Setna's twelve-year-old son, Se-Osiris, was a child wizard.

One day, Setna and Se-Osiris stood at the palace window watching two funeral processions. One was for a wealthy man who lay in a sarcophagus overlaid with gold. An army of mourners bore gifts for his tomb as they carried his mummy to its resting place. Priests walked ahead, chanting hymns and the words of power the man would need to get through the portals of the underworld. By contrast, the other funeral was the simple affair of a humble worker. His sons carried his body in an unassuming wooden coffin. His wife and his sons' wives were the only ones who mourned his passing.

"Hmmm," mused Setna, watching the two processions going down to the Nile River to the boats that would carry them across to the burial grounds. "I hope my passing is like that rich man's, with plenty of people to weep and the priests reminding me of all I need to know in Duat."

Se-Osiris thoughtfully replied, "Actually, I'm praying that your death will be like the poor man's."

Setna seemed crushed, but his son quickly explained. "What happens here, on this side of Duat, is irrelevant. It's what happens in the Hall of Truth that matters! I think the poor man will do better there than the rich man. I can prove it! Trust me. I know the magic spell to open the gates of Duat. I can release our souls, your ba and mine, to fly to the land of the dead. We can see the fates of these two men. This rich man has been evil all his life, but the poor man has been honest and good."

Nothing that his son said surprised Setna anymore. He knew they were taking a grave risk going into Duat. They could get stuck there in the land of the dead. Yet, Setna trusted Se-Osiris, so he agreed to go with him. They walked to the Temple of Osiris. As royalty, they were priests and could enter the sanctuary. Once they were inside, Setna locked the doors. They stood next to the idol of Osiris and the altar, and Se-Osiris drew a circle around it with them inside.

Se-Osiris threw powder three times on the small fire burning on the altar. The third time, a ball of fire exploded. As he spoke a magic spell, the temple shook, and the flame snuffed out, leaving them in the shadows. Yet, the temple was not completely dark. A light still came from the altar. What was it? Suddenly, horror paralyzed Setna. There he was! He and his son were standing on each side of the altar. How? He realized it was his ba, his soul, and that of Se-Osiris. A tongue of fire hovered over each shape.

Se-Osiris had the body of a large, golden-feathered bird but his own human head. The ba of Se-Osiris whispered softly, like a falling feather, yet the sound filled the temple. "Follow me, Father. The time is short. If we want to see Ra rise again over Egypt, we must be back in the land of the living by daybreak."

Setna forced his mouth to speak. He whispered, yet sound filled the temple. "I'm coming." Setna looked down to see he also had golden wings. The two spirits flew up to the temple's ceiling, which seemed to open and let them through to the sky. They flew to the west faster than an arrow shot by an Ethiopian archer.

The sun was setting, leaving the land in darkness except for a gash of red in the Western Desert. In front of them, Ra piloted his Ship of a Million Souls. All the souls who had died that day were in the boat on their way to the Hall of Truth. Setna and Se-Osiris flew after the vessel and into Duat. When the ship reached the Hall of Truth, all the souls got out of the ship, and Ra continued through the rest of the twelve chambers. The souls of Setna and Se-Osiris hovered over the newly dead souls at the door of the great hall.

The doorkeeper of the Hall of Truth challenged each soul as it approached. "Stay right there! I won't announce your entrance unless you know my name."

This was one of the things the Egyptians knew they needed to know before they died. They studied and memorized such facts in the Book of the Dead. Just to be safe, in case their soul forgot, many had a copy of the book buried with them for quick reference.

"Your name is Understander of Hearts and Searcher of Bodies," each soul answered—at least those who had properly prepared.

"To whom shall I announce you?" the doorkeeper queried.

"Tell the Interpreter of the Two Lands that I have arrived."

"Who is the Interpreter of the Two Lands?" asked the doorkeeper.

"He is Thoth, the god of wisdom."

One by one, the doorkeeper allowed each soul to pass into the Hall of Truth, where Thoth waited for them.

"What is the condition of your soul?" the ibis-headed Thoth asked each soul.

"It is pure," answered each soul.

"Shall I announce you to the one with a pavement of water, a ceiling of fire, and walls of living snakes?"

"Yes, he is Osiris," answered each soul. "Announce me to him."

Princess Nauny (second from left) in the Hall of Truth

Thoth led each soul to the green-skinned Osiris on his throne, still wrapped up as a mummy and holding a shepherd's crook. On the floor in front of him was a large scale. Anubis led each soul to the scale. Before he weighed their hearts, the souls spoke in their defense.

"I am pure! I come to you without guilt or sin. No one is here to accuse me. I live and eat truth. I have followed the laws of man and the gods. I have given proper worship and offerings to the gods and to the dead. I have fed the hungry, given water to the thirsty, and clothed the naked. Preserve me from Apep, the Eater of Souls. Protect me, Lord of Breath, great Osiris."

Setna and Se-Osiris watched as Anubis weighed each heart in the balance. "Look!" Se-Osiris said, nudging Setna. "There's the poor man we saw earlier! He passed the test. His heart has been found true and righteous. He's wearing fine robes and is on his way to the Field of Reeds!"

"Good for him!" Setna smiled. "But what happened to the rich man? I don't see him anywhere."

"Oh, he didn't make it this far! You remember the third gate we passed through on our way here?"

"Yes!" Setna shuddered. "It was horrible! That gate turned on a pivot, and the pivot was a wretched man's eye socket. I'll never forget his screams as the door opened."

Se-Osiris nodded. "That was him! That was the rich man. He is being punished for the pain and suffering he inflicted on people on Earth."

"And now," Se-Osiris warned, "We must hurry back to the Land of the Living. We must get there before the sunrise."

The two souls flew on their golden wings back to Thebes, into the Temple of Osiris, and back into their bodies. As father and son looked around, they saw pink and gold on the eastern horizon. Ra arose from Duat, and a new day dawned.

Chapter 6 Activity

Check your answers in the back of the book.

Egyptian Mythology: the Underworld

Across
3. Father of Se-Osiris
6. She ate souls whose hearts were heavy
8. Workforce in Duat

Down
1. She offered cool water in Duat
2. Jackal-headed god in Duat
4. Egyptian Underworld
5. God of the Dead and first mummy
6. Egyptian Paradise
7. Ghostlike creature, the smiter

Image source[42]

Chapter 7: The Pharaoh's Curse

The stories of ancient Egypt's pharaohs intertwine with myth. Almost everyone is familiar with the Egyptian pharaoh Tutankhamun—the young king around whom the myth of the pharaoh's curse has swirled. Curiously, this myth didn't emerge in ancient times but in the past century. Supposedly, a curse fell on anyone who disturbed his tomb. This chapter will unwrap the story of the curse and other mysteries of the child king.

What Do We Know about King Tutankhamun That Wasn't Myth?

Shortly after King Tut died, his successor, Horemheb, erased all the monuments and inscriptions referring to Tutankhamun and his father, Akhenaten. It wasn't that Horemheb had anything against King Tut personally. In fact, the two had been close in Tut's lifetime. Horemheb was the commander of Tut's armies. When the young king lost his temper, Horemheb calmed him down. Tut had no living children, so he named Horemheb his successor. So, why would Horemheb erase Tut?

Tutankhamun wasn't the problem. It was his father, Akhenaten, who had utterly disrupted Egypt's religious system by mandating that the Egyptians stop worshiping Isis, Ra, Thoth, and all the other gods. The Egyptians had been polytheistic for millennia. They had a deeply entrenched religious system and put their faith in it. If they did everything right, they could enter the Field of Reeds when they died. Everyone was appalled when Akhenaten upended the faith that was familiar to them, the faith that gave them comfort and hope in facing death.

As we discussed in chapter two, Akhenaten insisted on worshipping only one god, who didn't even have a proper name. This god was "The Aten," or the Sun Disk. Ra was the sun god, but Akhenaten's god was the actual sun everyone could see. However, Akhenaten said no one except him could actually worship the Aten.

Akhenaten, the heretic king[48]

"I'm the only one who can genuinely know and communicate with the Sun Disk," he said. "You cannot worship him directly because no one but me can access the Aten. Instead, you must worship me. I am his living incarnation. I am the Aten on Earth. Thus, everyone must pray to me, and I will pray to the Aten."

Of course, not everyone obeyed him. Yes, the temples to the other gods were shut down, and no one could publicly worship their images. But in the privacy of their homes, the Egyptians quietly kept the small idols of their old, familiar gods and continued to pray to them.

This "heresy," or deviation from Egypt's standard religion, is why Horemheb erased Akhenaten from Egypt's history. Akhenaten had disrupted Maat, putting Egypt in grave peril with the gods. Since Tutankhamun was Akhenaten's son, Horemheb erased his memory as well.

The one thing that Horemheb did not disturb was King Tut's tomb. Tutankhamun lay quietly in his grave for over 3,000 years. Horemheb may not have known where it was, as he was in Syria fighting the Hittites when Tut died. Although Horemheb was meant to be the next king, another official named Ay usurped the throne for a few years. Ay buried Tutankhamun in an unexpected place.

King Tutankhaten wasn't famous for anything he did as king. The only thing notable about his reign is that he reversed his father's policies and made Egypt officially polytheistic again. Tut was only nine when he became king, and he died ten years later. He never made it out of his teens. Furthermore, because Horemheb erased all memory of him, within decades, everyone had forgotten about him. He was the unknown king.

So, why is he so famous today? He is renowned for his mummy and tomb, which weren't discovered until the twentieth century CE. The tombs of other pharaohs had been raided and mostly emptied over the millennia, but Tut's tomb remained undisturbed until it was uncovered in 1922 CE. Within weeks, photographs of his sarcophagus and the treasures in his tomb circled the world in newspapers and magazines. Everyone was enthralled with the discovery of his lavish tomb. The newspapers also spoke of a curse that would fall on anyone who disrupted the king's grave. Could it be true?

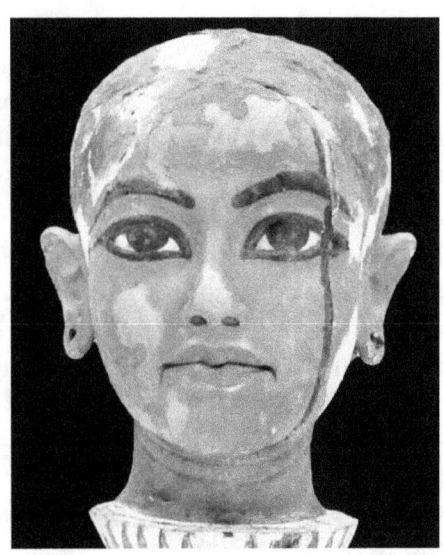

King Tut, the child king"

Before discussing whether King Tut's tomb was cursed, let's put several other mysteries to rest. For instance, what happened to his mother? Who or what killed her? Was Tutankhamun really disabled? How did he die at only nineteen years old? Why was he buried in such an unexpected place? Who else was in the grave with him? How did the world find out about this king whose record was erased?

Was King Tut's Mother Murdered?

We don't know the name of King Tut's mother, but we know that she was the full biological sister of his father, Akhenaten. Researchers had taken DNA samples from Tut's mummy and Akhenaten's mummy, which showed they were father and son. In the royal tombs, archaeologists found the mummy of a young, unnamed woman they called "The Younger Lady." She shared a tomb with Tiye, Akhenaten's mother. DNA sampling showed that The Younger Lady was Tiye's daughter, Akhenaten's sister, and Tut's mother. Tiye had several daughters, yet no one is sure which one The Younger Lady was.

Tut's mother suffered a violent death. Her mummy shows that a hard object struck her face, knocking a hole in her jaw and killing her. Scholars have tried to determine how she received the fatal wound. It might have been an accident. Maybe a horse kicked her. In that era, Egyptians used chariots; however, charioteers were mainly men involved in warfare and hunting. Nevertheless, artwork in Amarna showed Queen Nefertiti, Akhenaten's other wife, in a chariot. If Nefertiti used a chariot, it's possible that Tut's mother did too.

More likely, Tut's mother was the victim of palace politics. Akhenaten's chief wife was Nefertiti, his half-sister. She probably became co-pharaoh with him before he died and stayed on the throne for a year or two after his death. Nefertiti had six daughters with Akhenaten but no sons. Tutankhamun was seven when his father died. He was the king's only son and the heir to the throne. Usually, if a pharaoh was too young, his mother ruled as a regent in his place until he came of age. However, Nefertiti would not have wanted to release her power to her husband's other wife. She may have arranged the "accident" that killed Tut's mother.

No mention of Tutankhamun's mother appears on any inscriptions. No portraits of her have been found in his grave or elsewhere. Usually, a king's mother would have been a prominent person in his court. Analysis of his mother's mummy showed she was killed in her early twenties, probably around the time her husband died.

Maia, Tut's nurse and tutor, raised him. His regents were Horemheb, who handled the military, and Ay, who took care of administrative affairs.

Tut and Maia[46]

Was the Child King Disabled?

Some scholars insist that Tutankhamun was seriously disabled and couldn't walk without assistance. They theorize that his disability may have caused his death. Why do they think this? Over 100 walking sticks were in his grave, and Tut's left foot twisted in. However, most scholars say he could walk without problems. They think the tight wrappings twisted his foot after death. The long bones of Tut's legs showed no signs of unusual wear, as they would if he had a deformed foot. His shoes were buried with him and didn't show uneven wear either.

But why all the walking sticks? They were a status symbol. Tutankhamun likely carried them as fashion accessories, as men did in the Victorian era.

He did have mild scoliosis, or curvature of the spine, but many people have scoliosis without any significant problems. He also had bone necrosis in the two middle toes of his left foot, probably caused by a recent injury that could have healed naturally in time. If not, it could have been disabling as Tut aged.

Did Tut Die a Violent Death?

King Tut's left thigh bone was broken shortly before he died. Some researchers noted that the fracture's location suggests it broke while hitting the top rim of his chariot. During Tut's reign, his armies fought battles in Nubia (Sudan), Canaan (Israel and Palestine), and Syria. It's possible he went with them into battle and had a chariot accident or got hit in the thigh with some sort of weapon. Of course, an accident could have happened at home.

A broken bone usually isn't fatal unless it gets infected. Damage to internal organs, like his liver, may have occurred in the accident that broke his thigh. This is the most probable cause of his death. However, shortly after Tut's death, an epidemic struck the Hittites, who were fighting the Egyptians in Syria. The Hittites said they got sick from an illness the Egyptians brought. It killed the Hittite king, his crown prince, and much of the Hittite army. The Hittites reported that the epidemic continued in waves for about twenty years. Whatever the epidemic was, it likely started in Egypt. It may have killed King Tut, who was already weakened from his injury.

Another potential cause of Tut's death is malaria. The king's DNA showed he had malaria several times. He had the most severe type, which, even with today's modern medicine, causes over two million deaths in Africa annually.

When Did King Tutankhamun's Existence Come to Light?

As we mentioned, Horemheb went to great lengths to erase the memory of Tutankhamun and his father, Akhenaten, the religious heretic. The Egyptians kept scrupulous records of the reigns of their kings but left these two pharaohs off the king list.

However, Akhenaten had built a new city as his capital, called Akhetaten (or Amarna). The city didn't last long. Several years into his reign, Tut moved Egypt's capital to Memphis, near today's Cairo. Amarna became a ghost town. Eventually, the desert sands covered it, and everyone forgot about its existence.

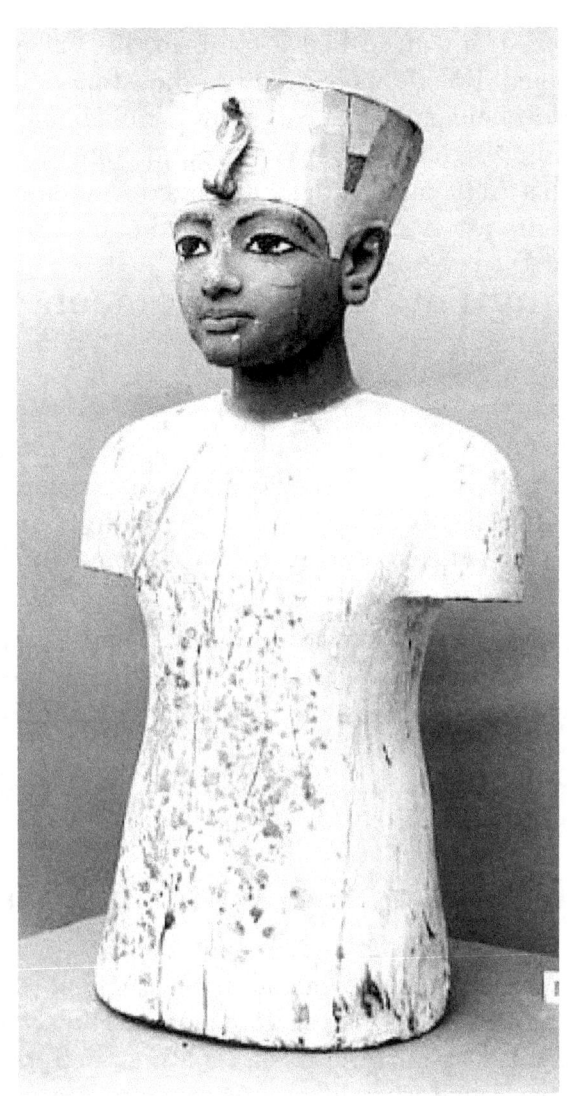

A carving of King Tut from his tomb[46]

In the late 1700s CE, Napoleon Bonaparte's army stumbled upon the ruins of the ancient city. This discovery led to ongoing explorations of the city, and archaeologists found the "Amarna Letters"—correspondence between Akhenaten and the kings of Babylon, Syria, and other places. It wasn't long before they found Akhenaten's tomb. His mummy wasn't there, as King Tut took the family mummies with him when he relocated his capital. Tutankhamun reburied them in the Valley of the Kings across the Nile from Thebes. After uncovering Amarna, archaeologists knew about Akhenaten.

In 1907 CE, a team unearthed a tomb in the Valley of the Kings, which they labeled KV55. The mummy they found in this tomb is almost certainly Akhenaten. The seal on the tomb contained inscriptions with Tutankhamun's name. This seal and other clues informed archaeologists that Akhenaten had a son named Tutankhamun, who was a king. The search was on to find the tomb of the mysterious king!

Was King Tut Buried in Someone Else's Tomb?

Yes. Construction had started on the tomb meant for Tutankhamun, but he unexpectedly died when he was only nineteen. His tomb wasn't ready yet. However, his advisor and successor, Ay, was an older man. He had already built his own tomb, so he had King Tut buried in it. During Ay's four-year reign, his workers completed what was meant to be Tut's tomb and buried Ay there.

When Ay built his tomb, he wasn't royalty. Typically, workers carved the royal tombs into the cliffs overlooking the Nile in the Valley of the Kings. That's where grave robbers focused their attention. But Ay's tomb was dug into the ground between two hills. A layer of sand soon covered the entrance to this modest, underground tomb. No one knew King Tut existed, and no one knew his tomb was there.

Who Was Buried with King Tut?

Tutankhamun and his wife, Ankhesenamun, had no living children. However, Ankhesenamun got pregnant twice. The first child, a little girl, died when her mother was six months pregnant. The second child, also a girl, died when Ankhesenamun was a month away from her due date. The baby may have died in childbirth or in the womb. Both of the tiny bodies were mummified and laid to rest in miniature gold-covered coffins. The sisters were placed together in a bigger wooden box. Tut believed they would be waiting for him in the Field of Reeds. When their father died, his two little daughters were tenderly laid in his grave.

How Was His Tomb Found?

Once archaeologists learned about a previously unknown king named Tutankhamun, they wondered where his tomb was. In 1907 CE, Lord Carnarvon of England paid for Howard Carter, an Egyptologist, to find the tomb. During World War I, Carter paused his search when Egypt was a war zone between the Ottoman Turks and the British. After the war, Carter resumed looking for Tut's grave.

He surveyed the royal tombs carved into the hills in the Valley of the Kings. So far, no new tombs had been found, and the old ones had already been investigated. Then, one of his workers fell over something. What tripped him? It turned out to be stairs leading down to an underground tomb. Carter was excited. No one expected to find a tomb entrance underground. Could it possibly be Tut's? When Lord Carnarvon got the news, he hurried to Egypt. He and Carter opened the grave in November 1922 to find Tutankhamun's sarcophagus surrounded by unimaginable treasures.

Was King Tut's Tomb Cursed?

The discovery of Tutankhamun's tomb was a media sensation. Journalists excitedly converged on the Valley of the Kings. Soon, newspapers circled the globe bearing lurid tales of a curse associated with the tomb. Headlines screamed, "Curse found at tomb's entrance: 'They who enter this sacred tomb shall be swiftly visited by the wings of death!'"

Was it true? Were Carter and his team cursed for opening the tomb?

Some of the pharaohs did inscribe curses on their tombs. One said that anyone who disturbed the pharaoh's rest would die of a disease that

The gold mask that covered King Tut's face⁴⁷

doctors couldn't diagnose. However, in the case of King Tut, it turns out the curse was Carter's ploy to keep curiosity seekers or grave robbers away from the tomb. Journalists happily ran with it because stories of a curse kept newspapers flying off the stands. And yet, several subsequent deaths made folks wonder if there really was a curse.

Three weeks after the tomb was opened, James Henry Breasted, another Egyptologist, arrived to help Carter sort and catalog the items in the tomb. Carter sent Breasted to his house to get something, and as he approached the house, Breasted heard a shrill scream. He entered to find a cobra holding Carter's canary in its mouth. The cobra represented Egyptian royalty. The *New York Times* ran with the story.

Four months after opening Tut's tomb, Lord Carnarvon dropped dead. While shaving, he had nicked a mosquito bite; he died three weeks later of blood poisoning. In early 1923, George Jay Gould, a wealthy railroad baron, also visited the tomb. He fell ill with a fever while in Egypt and died shortly after. Egyptologist Hugh Evelyn-White, who had assisted Carter in the tomb, committed suicide in 1924 after writing a note that he was under a curse.

Despite the handful of deaths, none of the Egyptian workers who assisted with digging the tomb or cataloging its treasures seemed affected. The rumor spread that the curse only applied to foreigners, not native Egyptians. This doesn't make sense. When Tut and other pharaohs were buried, the most likely grave robbers would have been Egyptians, not people from the other side of the world. The curse would have applied to Egyptians.

Fifty-eight people stood around the tomb when Carter and Carnarvon first opened it. Only eight of those people died in the next twelve years. Howard Carter lived for sixteen more years and died at age sixty-four. Lord Carnarvon's daughter, Lady Evelyn, entered the tomb just behind her father. She lived for another fifty-seven years. Most of the people involved lived for decades.

Chapter 7 Activity

Mark each question "T" or "F." Check your answers in the back of the book.

( ) 1. Tutankhamun wiped out all memory of his father, Akhenaten.

( ) 2. Tut's father, Akhenaten, forbade everyone to worship the Egyptian gods and goddesses.

( ) 3. Tut lived to age thirty.

( ) 4. Tut's mother died from a violent blow to her face.

( ) 5. Tut had a broken thigh bone when he died.

( ) 6. Tut was buried in a borrowed tomb.

( ) 7. Tut's teenage daughters were buried with him.

( ) 8. Tut's tomb was carved high up in the face of a cliff.

( ) 9. Lord Carnarvon died four days after opening Tut's tomb.

( ) 10. Over half the workers who opened Tut's tomb died in the next three years.

Chapter 8: The Sphinx and Other Monsters

In addition to about thirty major deities and over a thousand minor gods and goddesses, the ancient Egyptians also had monsters and mythical creatures. Apep was a monster, as was Ammit, who devoured lost souls. The Bennu bird was a mythical creature that brought good fortune. But how did they distinguish between these and their deities? Some gods and goddesses seemed rather monster-like in appearance and attitude. For instance, the spine-chilling goddess Ahti was an ill-natured hippo with the head of a wasp. She stung children, brought misfortune with her, and lacked any redeeming characteristics. And yet, the Egyptians considered her a deity. She probably fell into a category like Set, who was the god of chaos yet served a vital role in defending Ra from the evil serpent Apep.

The Egyptians didn't worship or pray to monsters and mythical creatures. Some were harmful to humans, while others were protectors or helpers. We've already discussed Apep, Ammit, and the Bennu bird. Let's check out some other monsters and mythical beings.

What Was a Sphinx?

A sphinx had a human head and a lion's body. The Greeks and Egyptians exchanged mythology as they interacted through trade and sometimes war. The Greek sphinx had wings and a woman's head. The Egyptian sphinx was wingless, and its head was usually an Egyptian king. The Greek sphinx was a scary creature that ate folks who couldn't figure out the riddle she gave them. In contrast, Egyptian sphinxes were strong and fierce males, and their role was protective. They represented royalty and the god Horus.

The ancient Egyptians built thousands of sphinx statues. Although the Great Sphinx of Giza often comes to mind, most sphinxes were only around six feet long. They decorated the walkways of temples and palaces. The nearly two-mile Avenue of Sphinxes connects the Luxor Temple with the Karnak Temple near Thebes. Over 800 sphinxes guard the road, along with ram statues and other creatures with a lion's body and a ram's head.

The Avenue of Sphinxes[48]

In the Old Kingdom, King Khafre built Egypt's second-largest pyramid in Giza. The Khafre Pyramid stood next to his father Khufu's pyramid, the largest in Egypt. Near his pyramid, Khafre's workers built the Great Sphinx, featuring Khafre's head. This statue is an astounding sixty-six feet high and 240 feet long. Its paws are twice as high as an average man.

What's more incredible is that the artisans carved it in place from a single mass of limestone. Egyptian laborers uncovered the massive chunk when quarrying stone for the pyramids. As they carved the limestone, they used the pieces they cut off to build a temple in front of the statue. The artisans painted the Great Sphinx red, blue, and yellow; however, the blowing desert sands wore most of the color off.

The Prince and the Buried Sphinx

Long ago lived a handsome prince of Egypt named Thutmose IV. His father was Pharaoh Amenhotep II. Although an older brother was the crown prince, Thutmose was his father's favorite. Thutmose's brothers were jealous of the attention their father lavished on him. They started an underhanded campaign to make Thutmose lose favor with his father, the priests, and the people of Egypt.

His brothers whispered that Thutmose wasn't cut out for leadership. "He has a mean streak!" they gossiped. "Yes, and he's too flashy!" another brother spoke up. "I heard he disrespects the gods." The brothers nodded. "Thutmose doesn't have what it takes to rule Egypt!"

Thutmose IV[49]

Thutmose tried to ignore the smear campaign. But when he heard about plots to kill him, he became depressed and fearful. To avoid palace politics, Thutmose began spending most of his time away from court. He was an avid sportsman and hunter. As an expert archer, he could shoot one arrow after another into the center of the target. He loved riding his chariot like the wind, chasing antelope over the desert sands. He would climb the cliffs rising from the Nile and hunt lions in their dens.

Egypt was celebrating the festival of Ra, and the royal family was staying in Memphis for the celebration. Thutmose wanted to escape all the pageantry. He longed to be back out in the endless desert. The next morning, he snuck out at dawn to hunt gazelle. After he had hunted for hours, the sun began to beat down. Ahead of him, he could see the three massive pyramids of Giza and the majestic statue rising out of the sand. "I'll rest here, in the shadow of the sphinx!"

In Thutmose's day, the Great Sphinx was over 1,000 years old. The Egyptians thought he was a god. They called him the Father of Terrors and offered sacrifices to him. When Thutmose looked up at the statue, all he saw was the head and neck of the sphinx. He didn't realize that its body was buried in the sand. Hot and exhausted, Thutmose sat in the shade under the sphinx's chin. He prayed for help against his enemies at court and quickly fell into a deep sleep.

As Thutmose slept, he dreamed. In his vision, the statue of the Great Sphinx stirred. It writhed and shook, trying to remove the sand covering most of its body. Thutmose looked up to see that the sphinx was no longer a stone statue but a living, breathing creature peering down at him. The sphinx spoke in a voice that resonated like thunder yet was gentle and kind. He talked to Thutmose as a father speaks to his child, calling himself Harmachis, a manifestation of the god Horus:

> "Look at me, my son Thutmose, Prince of Egypt! I am your father, Harmachis. I am the father of all the pharaohs of Egypt. It is your destiny to become the next pharaoh of Egypt. I ordain you to wear the Double Crown of the North and the South. You shall sit on Egypt's throne, and the world's people will come and kneel before you, bringing tribute. All of Egypt will be yours, along with health, strength, and a long life. You will never need anything, nor will you experience trouble. It's all yours! You just need to do one thing for me."

The Great Sphinx[50]

Thutmose was spellbound, listening to the Sphinx. What could this gigantic creature need from him? The sphinx continued:

> "Thutmose! This sand has overwhelmed me. It's covered me to my neck! It's smothering me. Hurry! Care for me like a good son honors his father. If you uncover me, my heart will incline toward you. Our spirits will intertwine. If you are a good son to me, I will always be with you, guiding you and leading you to greatness."

At this moment, Thutmose awoke from his dream. He gazed at the Great Sphinx. The desert sands surrounded the statue, up to its neck, like the waves on the sea. He responded:

> "My father, Harmachis! I swear before you and all of Egypt's gods. If I indeed become pharaoh, my first act will be to free you from the sand. I will build a temple to you and inscribe in stone your command and my fulfillment of it."

This myth probably contains an element of truth. Thutmose IV was an actual prince of Egypt who became pharaoh despite being a younger son. Did the dream really happen, or was it propaganda to legitimize his rule after usurping the throne from his older brother? Only the Great Sphinx knows!

However, Thutmose did unbury the Great Sphinx. He built a temple twelve feet high, right between the Sphinx's paws. In the back of the shrine was a fifteen-ton granite monument that told Thutmose's dream. The Great Sphinx might have helped Thutmose become pharaoh, but his promises of health and long life did not pan out. Thutmose IV died while still in his twenties.

Despite Thutmose's efforts to dig the Great Sphinx out of the sand, the desert reclaimed the statue in the following centuries. When the workers first carved the sphinx, they had to dig down into the sand to access the chunk of rock from which it was cut. Thus, it was below ground level when built around 2500 BCE. Although workers would have cleared away all the surrounding sand when they first built the sphinx, the desert winds inevitably blew it back.

By the time Egypt became part of the Roman Empire, the Great Sphinx was up to its neck again in sand! Around 50 CE, Emperor Nero ordered it to be dug out again. He built retaining walls around it to help prevent the sand from building up again. By the 1600s CE, drawings of the Great Sphinx show the sand was back up to its neck. In the late

1800s CE, an Italian crew dug it out, uncovering the Great Sphinx's chest and paws and the "Dream Stele" left by Thutmose IV, telling his dream.

The Great Sphinx with the Dream Stele between its front legs[51]

El Naddaha, Temptress of the Nile

El Naddaha was a creature with an enchanting woman's voice that called to men walking alone near the Nile at night. She even called them by name! The hapless man she called would walk closer to the river, curious to see who the woman was. He would finally fall in or be dragged to his death. Sometimes, people caught glimpses of the tall, beautiful woman, especially in the full moon. (This has happened even in recent times.) They described her as wearing a long, sheer, white dress, like those worn by ancient Egyptian women, with black hair cascading down her back. Folklore said she lived in an underwater cave on the banks of the Nile.

Because stories of El Naddaha cropped up in the mid-1900s CE, some people say she is a jinn, a spirit in Islamic mythology. However, ancient Greek mythology had sirens, whose voices lured sailors to their doom. Ancient Egypt had several water goddesses or spirits. For instance, Anuket was the goddess of the Nile River at the border of Egypt and Nubia. She wore a high headdress of reeds from the river, and she had a dark side. Her name meant "she who strangles." Anuket was sometimes associated with Hathor, who got drunk on the blood of men.

The Griffin

The griffin was a mythological creature in many cultures, including ancient Iraq, Persia, and Greece. The Egyptians portrayed griffins with the body of a lion and an eagle's head and wings. Sometimes, the pharaoh was painted as a griffin with the bodies of Egypt's enemies under his claws. Other times, griffins pulled the pharaoh's chariot or walked on a leash led by a human. The Egyptians considered the griffin to be a protector from evil incantations. Griffins also guarded treasures and kept secrets. Because Horus had a falcon head, he was often associated with griffins.

An Egyptian griffin[52]

The **hieracosphinx** was quite similar to a griffin. It had a lion's body and a falcon head but no wings. This creature was strongly associated with Horus and was pictured wearing the crown of Egypt.

Egyptian writings mentioned a creature called ***Akhekh***. He was either an ally of Set, the god of chaos, or a form that Set took. Akhekh is a monster of the water and chaos. Scholars debate what this creature looked like. Some think it was the griffin or a lion with wings. Others believe it was a winged antelope with a vulture head. The Akhekh symbolized terror, and it had a booming roar. Ramesses the Great was compared to an Akhekh as he terrorized the Hittites in the Battle of Kadesh.

The Serpopard

What do you get if you cross a long-necked dinosaur with a leopard? A serpopard! It had a leopard body and head (without the spots) and a long, snake-like neck. Serpopards almost always appeared in pairs.

The serpopard featured in Egyptian art from the Pre-Dynastic to the Old Kingdom eras. A carving of this weird creature shows up in the Narmer Palette. Narmer was the first king of unified Egypt in the Old Kingdom. The Narmer Palette was a two-foot piece of flat stone carved on both sides. One side had two serpopards with intertwining necks, representing the union of Upper and Lower Egypt. This creature also appeared in artwork in southern Iran and Iraq between 4000 and 3000 BCE.

Two serpopards on the Narmer Palette[58]

Uraeus, the Rearing Cobra of the Pharaohs

With her cobra hood dilated, the gold figure of Uraeus coils on the king's head. Her head is reared over his brow, poised to strike. If someone threatened the pharaoh, she spit fiery poison from her eyes. Uraeus symbolized the ancient serpent goddess Wadjet, who the Egyptians first worshiped in the Nile Delta region in Predynastic times. One of her duties was ensuring that Ra's orders were carried out. She was the guardian of the king and his family and represented royalty. When the king wore the Uraeus head ornament, he had Wadjet's protection, authority, and legitimacy. Eventually, artwork showed the Egyptian queens and some gods wearing the Uraeus.

Uraeus coiled on the forehead of Pharaoh Seti I[54]

Chapter 8 Activity

Can you figure out who each description is talking about? Check the answers in the back of the book if you need help.

1. _____: She lured men to their deaths in the Nile River.

2. _____: He had a lion's body and an eagle's head and wings.

3. _____: It had a leopard's body and head and a long neck like a snake.

4. _____: He had a lion's body and a king's head.

5. _____: She was a cobra that adorned the king's head and protected him.

Chapter 9: Myths of Justice and Love

Not all of ancient Egypt's mythology was about gods and goddesses. The Egyptians loved stories about ordinary people caught up in the quest for justice. Other tales highlighted the endurance of true love. Of course, the gods usually got involved, but they weren't the main characters. The persistence, persuasiveness, and audacity of the people in these myths, when the odds were against them, won the admiration of the Egyptians.

The Eloquent Peasant

In the turbulent times between the Old Kingdom's end and the Middle Kingdom's beginning, there lived a poor salt trader named Khun-Anup. He had a hard life, with few possessions. However, he had two valuable assets. The first was tenacity; he doggedly pursued justice even when it was initially denied him. The second was the ability to argue his case boldly and eloquently.

Khun-Anup lived with his wife and children in the Salt Country near the Faiyum Oasis. He would load salt and natron (a chemical used to dry and preserve things) on his donkeys to trade in the city of Henenseten. On his way, he had to pass through the lands of the High Steward, Meruitensa. The steward's overseer was Tehuti-nekht, a greedy and evil man. In those days, Egypt didn't have clear laws about roads and the right-of-way. Tehuti-nekht's cornfield had encroached on the road, leaving only a narrow strip along the canal.

As Tehuti-nekht watched Khun-Anup approaching with his donkeys laden with goods, he concocted an evil plan. He would steal the donkeys and what they carried. The donkeys could barely navigate the narrow path between the canal and the fields. Tehuti-nekht made it even more difficult by spreading a shawl over the road. When Khun-Anup's donkeys traveled along the canal, they trampled on the shawl. It was either that or go into the river or the cornfield.

Workers plow a field as a donkey caravan passes in this tomb painting.[55]

"Stop!" yelled Tehuti-nekht, his face red with anger. "How dare you drive your animals over my clothes?"

"I'll try to go around," Khun-Anup cheerfully answered. He guided his donkeys to the side of the path, into the corn.

"What? Now your donkeys are trampling through my corn!" raged Tehuti-nekht.

"Well, I have no choice!" Khun-Anup snapped back. "Your shawl is blocking the path. It's either walk on the shawl or walk in the cornfield."

As the two men exchanged words, one of the donkeys began munching on the corn.

"Look!" Tehuti-nekht screamed. "Your donkey is eating my corn! That's theft! You must give me that donkey in payment for the corn he ate."

"That's robbery!" Khun-Anup retorted. "These lands belong to the High Steward, Meruitensa. I'll discuss this with him! He'll not let you get by with this!"

"Ha! Do you think he'll listen to you? You're a nobody!" Tehuti-nekht beat Khun-Anup and stole all his donkeys. For an entire day, Khun-Anup wept, begging Tehuti-nekht to return his donkeys, to no avail.

"I'm wasting my breath! I'm going to find Lord Meruitensa." Khun-Anup stalked into Henenseten.

Khun-Anup tracked down the High Steward. He bowed with his face to the ground in front of him. "I have a grievance," Khun-Anup said. He explained the issue with Tehuti-nekht. Meruitensa allowed him to present his case to the nobles in the Hall of Justice. Khun-Anup's eloquence deeply moved the steward. Nevertheless, the judges refused to consider the poor man's case. Meruitensa went to the king to discuss the case.

"Put it all down in writing," the king said. "I want to read what this well-spoken man has to say. Also, make sure he and his family have food to eat while he's arguing his case since he's lost his livelihood. But don't tell him where it's coming from!"

For nine days straight, Khun-Anup trudged into the Hall of Justice and pleaded his case before the magistrates. At first, they ignored them. Then, they got exasperated and had him beaten, but he wouldn't give up. Meruitensa brought the papyrus scrolls with Khun-Anup's petitions to the king. The king was so charmed with his poetic speech and unabashed sense of justice that he permitted Meruitensa to pronounce judgment. Meruitensa stripped Tehuti-nekht of his position and lands. He gave Khun-Anup the lands and made him his new overseer.

The Pharaoh and Helen

This spin on the Trojan War takes place in the New Kingdom. The Greek historian Herodotus wrote it down in the 400s BCE. As a young man, he spent time in Egypt, gathering stories and histories of Egypt. Presumably, this was an older myth he collected from the Egyptians, as it correctly recorded details about the pharaoh's names and their understanding of the soul. It also correctly identifies Helen as being from Sparta, *not* Troy.

At one time, the Trojan War and Helen were all considered pure myth. However, archaeological digs have uncovered the city of Wilusa on Turkey's northwestern coast. The Greek poet Homer, who wrote about the Trojan War in the 8th century BCE, said Wilusa was another name for Troy. Hittite records say it was part of their extended empire. The city was built and destroyed several times, with a new city built on the ruins of the earlier ones. One layer of Troy was destroyed around 1180 BCE, which coincides with the time the Greeks say the war ended (and also matches the dates of the Egyptian kings in this story).

This myth begins in the days of Pharaoh Seti II, who ruled from around 1203 to 1200 BCE. A storm drove a large ship from the north to Egypt, and its sailors harbored in the mouth of the Nile. Thonis, the Egyptian governor of that region, learned the sailors were from Greece. They told him they wanted to desert their ship and seek refuge in Egypt.

"Why?" asked Thonis.

"We fear the wrath of our gods if we stay on that ship. The prince on this ship carried off the wife of Sparta's king!"

Thonis placed the Spartan queen, Helen, in the temple of Hathor for her protection while he sorted out the affair. He then escorted the prince to King Seti, who politely greeted him.

Seti II[56]

"Welcome to Egypt! Thonis tells me you are the son of a king. What country are you from?"

The prince bowed to Seti. "I come in peace, my Lord. The god Poseidon sent a storm that drove us off course. My father is Priam, king of Troy. I was returning there after a visit to Greece, where I met the most beautiful woman in the world and won her as my wife. Her name is Helen of Sparta, daughter of King Tyndareus."

Pharaoh Seti frowned. "Tell me, prince, just how did you win Helen? Are the Greek kings in the habit of sending their daughters over the sea to marry princes of other lands? Isn't Troy a long distance from Greece? And aren't the two lands at war right now?"

"Greece and Troy fought some battles in my grandfather's day, but we are presently at peace. I was among many other princes who went to Sparta to win Helen's hand. Her father chose me."

At this point, the sailors of the Greek ship began angrily muttering among themselves. Seti turned to them. "Speak up! Don't be afraid."

"Oh king, we are Greeks, not Trojans. This man, Prince Paris, did come to Greece on friendly terms. However, Helen's father did *not* choose him! Long before Prince Paris arrived, he chose Prince Menelaus as her husband. Menelaus and Helen have been married for several years. While Menelaus was away, Paris kidnapped Helen and carried her to our ship. The gods sent the storm that landed us here."

"Not true!" Paris cried out. "Helen came with me of her own free will. She hated her husband!"

Seti cleared his throat. "Well, Prince of Troy. Which is the truth? First, you told me her father chose you. Then you admitted she was already married."

Seti sent Paris to the royal guesthouse under the close watch of his guards. "Now! Let's visit this Greek princess at the Temple of Hathor," said Seti.

When he met Helen, he realized she truly was the most beautiful woman in the world. She told the pharaoh that she was happily married to Menelaus. They had two children.

"I have no love for Paris, Prince of Troy," she said adamantly.

Helen of Sparta[87]

After hearing Helen's version of events, Seti mused. "I know what happened. Paris shapeshifted into the image of your husband to lure you away from your palace and to his ship. Our magicians here do it all the time."

"Really?" asked Helen. "In Greece, only the gods can shapeshift. But we don't have as much magic there as you do here."

Helen fell to her knees before Seti, weeping. "Please let me stay here under your protection until my loving husband finds me. Don't let Paris carry me as his captive to Troy!"

Her words moved Seti, who promised, "You may stay here in the Temple of Hathor, where you will live in honor until Menelaus comes for you. I'll send this evil Paris away."

Seti informed Paris he must leave Egypt by sunrise the following day. At first, Paris raged and blustered. However, he obediently set sail for Troy in the early morning hours. Strangely, he thought Helen was with him. What happened? Seti's daughter, Tausret, was the High Priestess of Hathor. While worshiping the goddess, the temple rumbled, and a brilliant light shone behind her. When she turned, she saw Thoth, the god of wisdom.

"Don't be afraid. I come with a message from the high god Amun-Ra. He says you will one day be Queen of Egypt. But tonight, you must witness what's about to happen, so you can tell Helen's husband when he comes. Amun-Ra, whom the Greeks worship as Zeus, says that the Greeks and Trojans will fight a ten-year war for Helen. Troy's destruction will end the war. However, Helen will really be here until her husband, Menelaus, arrives. She won't be in Troy. Only her Ka will be there. I will draw out her spirit tonight; everyone will think it's her. But they will only see her Ka."

Tausret watched Thoth walk toward Helen's room. Shortly after, he walked by with Helen. Only, it wasn't Helen. It was her ghost, her Ka. They passed through the temple's closed doors into the night. When they reached the ship, Thoth transformed into the Greek god Hermes and handed Helen's Ka to Paris. The Trojan prince was overjoyed. He immediately set sail for Troy.

The real Helen stayed in Egypt, in the Temple of Hathor. Many Egyptians thought she was an incarnation of the goddess and called her the "foreign Hathor." Seti died soon after, and his son Siptah became pharaoh. Because he was still a child, his older sister, Tausret, high priestess of Hathor, ruled as his regent. Siptah died about six years later, and Tausret ruled as queen until a relative named Setnakht stole the throne. He only ruled for four years before he died, and his son, Ramesses III, became pharaoh.

Queen Tausret[88]

Through all these years, while civil war rocked Egypt and the Trojan War raged across the seas, Helen lived in the Temple of Hathor. She didn't seem to age. She still had the beautiful face that launched a thousand ships. The pharaohs honored her as Seti had. But then, Ramesses III came to the throne. He announced he planned to make Helen his queen. Tausret was still alive, and she tried to talk Ramesses III out of his plan.

"Seti, Siptah, Setnakht, and I all swore an oath! We promised to protect Helen until her husband returned. Remember, she *does* have a husband. You can't legally marry her!"

Ramesses decided to postpone the wedding until he could discover if Helen's husband, Menelaus, were still alive. He asked his magicians to see what they could find out. A few days later, a shipwrecked sailor came to the Temple of Hathor and knelt in prayer. Tausret was still the High Priestess, and she approached the foreign sailor, asking him why he came to the temple.

"I had a dream!" the man answered. The god Hermes, the one you call Thoth, told me to come here and find the Foreign Hathor and tell her everything."

"Well, then, start speaking," said Tausret. "The Foreign Hathor is behind you, out of sight, but she can hear what you say."

"I am Menelaus, the King of Sparta. Paris stole my wife, but I got her back when Troy fell. After Troy burned, the storms blew my ships all over the seas. Finally, I came here with my lovely Helen, my wife. As we sailed into the Nile, a storm struck and sank my ship, but Helen and I swam to an island. We slept in a cave, but when I woke the next morning, she was gone without a trace! I searched for her the entire day but couldn't find her. I'm afraid a crocodile carried her off. I fought for ten years to get her back. I can't bear the thought of losing her again!"

"King of Sparta," spoke Tausret. "The gods' will has been done. Paris brought Helen here years ago when a storm drove him to Egypt. Helen has been here all along, living in honor and safety until you came for her."

"How can that be?" gasped Menelaus. "I rescued Helen in Troy and carried her away. We were together until she disappeared from the island. How could she have been here all those years?"

"You only saw her Ka, her spirit form," explained Tausret. "Helen is here!"

Tausret pulled back the curtains of a small shrine to reveal Helen, who ran with outstretched arms to her husband. Menelaus enfolded Helen in his arms, touching her face to see if it were really her. "Oh, my dearest Helen! Were you here all those years? We fought and died for a spirit! The Egyptian magic is greater than we realized!"

Menelaus and his friend Patroclus, who died in the Trojan War[59]

"My love!" said Helen. "We're not out of danger yet. The new pharaoh, Ramesses III, wants to marry me. I think he will force me even if I refuse him."

Tausret spoke up. "I'll do everything I can to help you two escape Egypt. But no harm must come to Ramesses."

The three concocted a daring scheme. When Ramesses arrived, he found Helen dressed in mourning clothing. Tausret tried to comfort her as Menelaus stood to the side, still ragged and unshaven after his shipwreck.

"What happened?" Ramesses demanded.

Tausret explained, pointing to Menelaus. "This man is a shipwrecked sailor from Troy. Helen's husband, Menelaus, was on the same ship. He did not survive. This sailor saw him dead and carried away by the waves."

"Well then, Helen!" Ramesses crowed. "That means nothing stands between our marriage!"

"Only my husband's memory," Helen murmured as tears streamed down her face.

"But it's been so many years! How can you still grieve?" asked Ramesses.

"He was my husband and a great man! I must mourn him properly so his spirit will rest in Hades. Please, let me give him the rites that are due him."

"Of course!" said Ramesses. "Your wish is my command. I know nothing about Greek funeral customs, so please tell me."

"I need a ship," said Helen. "It should have wine and food for the funeral banquet. We need a bull to sacrifice to my husband's spirit. These Greek sailors will go with me because they know our funeral customs. I will make a final offering to my husband's spirit. But we must do it at sea because that is where his spirit is. Once I have mourned and given him the proper rites, I can be your wife."

"Of course, of course!" said Ramesses eagerly.

So Menelaus, his sailors, and Helen got into a ship with the sacrificial bull. The ship sailed up the Nile and out to sea. Later, Ramesses discovered he had been tricked. The ship never returned. Helen and her lawful husband were on their way back to Greece. Ramesses was angry and disappointed, but Thoth appeared to him, telling him it was Amun-Ra's will. Ramesses bowed and accepted that Helen would not be his wife.

Chapter 9 Activity

Choose the correct answer for each blank from the list below. The answers are in the back of the book.

Tehuti-nekht took Khun-Anup's _____ when one of them ate some corn in the evil overseer's field. Khun-Anup went to the Hall of Justice to plead his case. His _____ moved the High Steward, _____. However, the judges dismissed his case. For _____ straight days, he argued his case until he finally received _____.

_____, a prince of Troy, stole _____ from her husband. A shipwreck brought them to Egypt, where she sought protection from the pharaoh, _____. She hid out in the Temple of _____ with the pharaoh's daughter _____. The god Thoth separated her ____ from her body, and her spirit went to Troy with Paris while her body stayed in Egypt. She was safe until the new pharaoh, _____, wanted to marry her. Fortunately, her husband arrived, the victim of another _____, and she was able to escape with him.

donkeys	eloquence	Hathor
Helen	justice	Ka	Meruitensa
nine	Paris	Ramesses III
Seti II	shipwreck	Tausret

Chapter 10: Myths of Maidens and Magicians

The myths in this chapter involve three Egyptian kings and their interactions with magic and lovely young ladies. Two stories are set in the Old Kingdom, yet they were written 800 years later on the Westcar Papyrus. They showcase the miracles of court magicians, who the Egyptians firmly believed had supernatural powers. The third is a story recorded by the Greek historians Herodotus and Strabo. It is a Cinderella story about a young woman and the last great pharaoh before the Persians took over Egypt in 525 BCE.

The Girl Who Lost Her Necklace in the Lake

King Sneferu was bored. He had no wars at the moment. He had successfully raided Libya and Nubia, enslaving thousands and capturing 20,000 cattle, goats, and sheep. His architects were experimenting with building the first true pyramids with pointy tops and smooth sides. The first one collapsed before it was finished. Folks called the second one the "bent" pyramid because the architects didn't quite get the angles right. Now, his architects were building the "red" pyramid, assuring him that this one would turn out fine. With no pressing matters of state, Sneferu invited his chief magician, Zazamankh, to entertain him.

Sneferu complained. "I've walked through every room in my palace, trying to find something to do. I know you can always conjure up ways to entertain me!"

"You need to go sailing!" Zazamankh suggested.

"I've often sailed the Nile and the lake south of Memphis. I'm weary of that."

"You won't be bored with the sailing expedition I have in mind!" Zazamankh promised. "Your rowers will be the prettiest maidens in your harem! They'll wear golden nets with their hair flowing down and be draped with jewels. You'll be captivated by their beauty and with the lovely trees and birds around the lake."

"All right, you've sold me!" Sneferu smiled. "Make it happen!"

A figure of a chief magician in the Egyptian court[60]

His magician ordered twenty ebony oars with gold and electrum inlay. Twenty young ladies, draped in gold net and jewels, rowed Sneferu about the shimmering lake. As they sang, he admired the flowers and birds. Sneferu was so enchanted that he felt he'd been transported to the future when Osiris rises from Duat to rule the earth again.

And then, it happened. The girl sitting in the stern was steering, and her oar caught on her necklace and flung it into the water. "My lotus necklace!" she cried out.

Leaning over, she looked into the water and saw it on the bottom of the lake.

"Keep rowing!" Sneferu commanded. "I'll get you another necklace."

"But I want *that* one!" She sobbed. "It was my favorite necklace!"

Sneferu groaned. The only person who could fix this was Zazamankh. "This whole outing was his idea! Someone get Zazamankh!"

So, his bodyguard in an accompanying boat fetched the magician, and Sneferu explained the problem. "This maiden's necklace fell into the lake and is at the bottom, twenty feet down. Now, she won't sing or steer the boat! I've promised her she can have any necklace from my treasury, but she only wants this one with the lotuses! I want to see joy in her eyes again. What can you do?"

"For someone with my skill set, this is easy!" Zazamankh assured the king. He leaned over and began chanting and waving his wand over the water. Suddenly, it seemed as if a giant knife had sliced the water. Zazamankh moved the water aside, and the boat slipped down to the lake bottom. With a cry of glee, the maiden reached over, grabbed her treasured necklace, and hung it on her neck again.

Zazamankh lowered his wand, and the lake water slowly moved back into place, lifting the boat to the surface. The maidens began rowing again, singing a love song as the glow of the setting sun reflected on the surface of the lake.

An Egyptian necklace of lotus blossoms[61]

King Khufu and Djedi the Magician

Sneferu's son, Khufu, was the next king. He was the one who built the Great Pyramid of Giza, the highest pyramid in the world. One day, Khufu's son told him about a magician living in Djed-Snofru.

"He's called Djedi," Hordjedef said. "They say he's over 100 years old. I've heard that if someone cuts off an animal's head, he can reattach it! They also say he can tame lions, so they walk around on a leash. Oh, and he's supposed to know how many secret chambers are in Thoth's temple!"

"Sound's intriguing!" Khufu said. "Bring him to the palace. I want to see if he can really do these things!"

When the magician arrived, Khufu said, "I've heard you can reattach a severed head." He pointed to a heavily-guarded man. "He's a condemned criminal. I'll have my executor cut off his head. Then you can reattach it!"

"No! I won't do that!" Djedi exclaimed. "My magic never involves human suffering."

"We're going to cut off his head anyway! He's been sentenced to die. You'll be saving him if you can really reattach heads."

"That's your business," Djedi insisted. "I won't have any part in it! But if you bring in some animals, I'll show you what I can do."

So Khufu ordered some animals brought in. His servants cut the head off a goose and put its body on one side of the room and the head on the other. Suddenly, the two parts moved together as Djedi chanted an incantation. The head reattached, and the goose jumped up, flapping his wings and honking. His men cut the heads off of a duck and a bull. Djedi put their heads back on, and the animals lived again.

"Amazing!" Khufu gasped in wonder. "So, how many secret rooms are in Thoth's temple?"

"I'm not sure how many there are, but I know *where* they are," Djedi answered. "However, the gods have ordained that only one person can enter the rooms. He hasn't been born yet. He will be the oldest son of triplets born to the woman Rededjet."

"Who's Rededjet?" Khufu asked.

"She is in the future. She will be the wife of the High Priest of Ra in the time of your great-grandson."

Khufu arranged accommodations for Djedi in the palace of his son Hordjedef and supplied the magician with an abundance of food and beer for the rest of his life.

The Girl with the Rose-Red Slippers

Cyrus the Great's Persian Empire threatened to swallow up Egypt, so Pharoah Amasis II encouraged Greeks to join his military as paid mercenaries. He also gave the city of Naucratis to the Greeks. Located on the westernmost branch of the Nile, near the Mediterranean Sea, it was a major trade center and a place for the Greek mercenaries to live. A wealthy Greek merchant named Charaxos lived in Naucratis.

One day, he passed the slave market and noticed a large crowd assembled. He wondered what was happening, so he pushed his way to the front. There, on the platform, was a girl more lovely than any he had ever seen. He could tell she was Greek, so he decided to buy her and set her free. Once he had taken her away from the market, he learned her story. Her name was Rhodopis, and she was from northern Greece. When she was a little girl, pirates raided her town and captured her. They took her to the island of Samos and sold her to a wealthy man who had many enslaved people. Her master sent her to Naucratis when she grew up, knowing her beauty would bring a great price.

Rhodopis's exquisite appearance captivated Charaxos. He built her a beautiful house with an open-air courtyard and a pool in its center. He lavished her with gifts, including rose-red slippers, which were her pride and joy. One day, she was bathing in the pool in the heat of the day. Suddenly, an eagle dove out of the sky, swooping into her courtyard. Before Rhodopis realized what was happening, it snatched up one of her rose-red slippers. Holding it in his talons, he soared up into the air.

Rhodopis couldn't believe her eyes. Why would the eagle want her red slipper? Surely, she would never see it again. She wept bitterly as she loved the slippers. She didn't know the eagle represented the god Horus, who seemed to be manipulating events. The eagle flew straight to the palace, where Pharaoh Amasis was holding court. The sound of flapping wings distracted Amasis, and he looked up to see an eagle flying toward him! When the eagle was a few feet away, he dropped a red slipper in the pharaoh's lap and disappeared into the sky.

Amasis II[62]

Once he recovered from the shock, Amasis looked down at the slipper in his lap. He admired its exquisite handiwork. "If the girl who wore this is as beautiful as this tiny slipper, she must be the world's loveliest woman. I want her for my harem!"

Amasis sent messengers throughout the land to find the owner of the slipper brought to him by Horus. When they reached Naucratis, they heard about Charaxos and the stunning Greek girl. "She never goes anywhere without these red slippers he bought her!"

They went to Rhodopis's house and showed her the red slipper. Rhodopis cried out in delight. "That's my slipper! An eagle took it! I never thought I'd see it again. One moment, I'll get the other one."

Moments later, Rhodopis reappeared with her red slipper, and the messengers saw it was an exact match. They fit her perfectly. "Come with us!" they said. "Horus took your slipper to the pharaoh. King Amasis wants you to join his harem."

Charaxos was heartbroken to lose Rhodopis but happy for her. The gods must have ordained it, considering the extraordinary events. When Amasis saw Rhodopis, he thought he was looking at a goddess. She would not be one of the many concubines in his harem. He made her his Great Royal Wife, and they enjoyed a marriage of love and happiness.

Chapter 10 Activity

These words come from the entire book. Check your answers in the back.

Word Search

```
A O H Q L X A S F Y H O R U S
S K H E P R I P R E A M M I T
E K Q K V E D H R I Q C V T O
T Z S F H R P I G O U I K V A
P H A T H U L N D S Y A P R O
A R H Z N A F X U I Y P D R P
U A I Y A L T U A R C E K H K
R J A A R M J H T I E P B O S
U Z B U D W A I O S Y I A D D
S C N E W A M N N R Y Q B O J
O V D I N X N K K E U R J P E
D P W M S B I U D H U G P I D
T H O T H I E Y B H T E G S I
M A A T J T S N M I X J T M D
M L E O Y B R E Y S S I O P W
```

Zazamankh	Rhodopis	Benben	Isis
Hathor	Osiris	Khepri	Duat
Anubis	Khufu	Sphinx	Auru
Horus	Thoth	Ammit	Set
Djedi	Maat	Apep	Ra

Image source[63]

Answer Key to Roundup Activities

Chapter 1 Answers

1. Benben
2. Geb
3. Great Cackler
4. Hathor
5. Maat
6. Nun
7. Nut
8. Ogdoad

A. Eight Deities of Creation **(8. Ogdoad)**
B. Eye of Ra **(4. Hathor)**
C. God of the earth **(2. Geb)**
D. Goddess of the sky and the heavenly cow **(7. Nut)**
E. Goddess (and concept) of cosmic order **(5. Maat)**
F. Goose that laid the cosmic egg **(3. Great Cackler)**
G. Island that rose out of the water at creation **(1. Benben)**
H. Primeval, chaotic ocean **(6. Nun)**

Chapter 2 Answers

(T) 1. Ra's daytime solar barque was called "Boat of a Million Years."

(T) 2. Duat was the Egyptian Underworld.

(F) 3. The Tree-covered Mountain was the Egyptian idea of Paradise. (Field of Reeds)

(F) 4. Apep was an elephant god. (serpent)

(T) 5. Some myths say Ra became a scarab-beetle at sunrise.

(F) 6. Monotheism is the worship of many gods. (one god)

(F) 7. Khepri was a falcon. (a scarab beetle)

(T) 8. The Bennu bird looked like a heron and symbolized rebirth.

(T) 9. The phoenix buried his father at Ra's Temple of the Sun in Heliopolis.

(T) 10. The Egyptians thought that Ra influenced the actions of the Mnevis Bull.

Chapter 3 Answers

1. I became the god of Duat, the Underworld.   (F. Osiris)
2. I was considered the mother of all pharaohs.   (D. Isis)
3. I was the destructive god of chaos and storms.   (G. Set (Seth))
4. I was Set's wife and the "Friend of the Dead."   (E. Nephthys)
5. I was the sky god, son of Osiris and Isis.   (C. Horus)
6. I was a cat-headed goddess.   (A. Bastet)
7. I was Maat's husband and god of wisdom.   (I. Thoth)
8. I was the god of the Nile Flood.   (B. Hapi)
9. I was the crocodile god of the military.   (H. Sobek)

Chapter 4 Answers

1. Who murdered Osiris?
   b. Set
2. Where did Isis find her dead husband?
   a. Byblos
3. How long did Set and Horus struggle over Egypt's throne?
   d. Eighty years
4. Who won the Battle of the Hippos?
   c. Neither
5. Who finally decided who would rule Egypt?
   b. Geb

Chapter 5 Answers

The Horus on the Crocodiles Stela had inscriptions and stories about treating scorpion stings and snakebites with magic and medicine. A carving of the little boy Horus on the monument showed him holding scorpions, snakes, an antelope, and a lion in his hands. The monument tells the story of how wicked Uncle Set sent a scorpion to sting baby Horus. When Isis called out to Ra for help, he stopped the sun in the sky and sent Thoth down to help. He chanted incantations to heal little Horus. Isis merged with the goddess Serket to become the Scorpion Goddess . Thoth assigned seven scorpions to protect Isis from Set and other dangers. But the scorpions got mad at a woman who refused to help Isis. They disobeyed Isis and stung the son of the woman. Isis forgave the woman and took pity on her son. She used her magic to heal him. The woman was sorry for not inviting Isis into her home. She gave treasures to Isis and to the poor old woman in the village who had been kind to the goddess.

Chapter 6 Answers

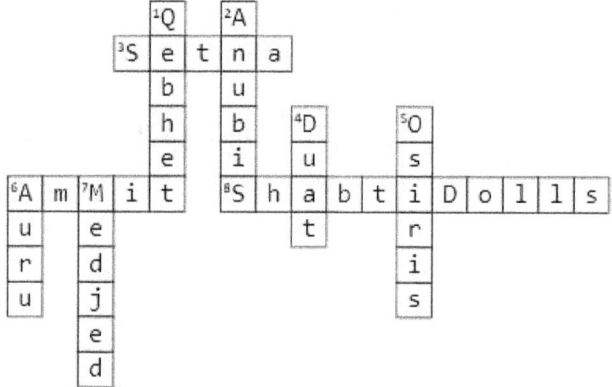

Across
3. Father of Se-Osiris
6. She ate souls whose hearts were heavy
8. Workforce in Duat

Down
1. She offered cool water in Duat
2. Jackal-headed god in Duat
4. Egyptian Underworld
5. God of the Dead and first mummy
6. Egyptian Paradise
7. Ghostlike creature, the smiter

Chapter 7 Answers

(F) 1. Tutankhamun wiped out the memory of his father, Akhenaten. (Horemheb did)

(T) 2. Tut's father, Akhenaten, forbade everyone to worship the Egyptian gods and goddesses.
(F) 3. Tut lived to age thirty. (19)
(T) 4. Tut's mother died from a violent blow to her face.
(T) 5. Tut had a broken thigh bone when he died.
(T) 6. Tut was buried in a borrowed tomb.
(F) 7. Tut's teenage daughters were buried with him. (fetuses or newborn babies)
(F) 8. Tut's tomb was carved high up in the face of a cliff. (underground)
(F) 9. Lord Carnarvon died four days after opening Tut's tomb. (four months)
(F) 10. Over half the workers who opened Tut's tomb died in the next three years.

Chapter 8 Answers

1. **El Naddaha**: She lured men to their deaths in the Nile River.
2. **Griffin**: He had a lion's body and an eagle's head and wings.
3. **Serpopard**: It had a leopard's body and head and a long neck like a snake.
4. **Sphinx**: He had a lion's body and a king's head.
5. **Uraeus**: She was a cobra that adorned the king's head and protected him.

Chapter 9 Answers

Tehuti-nekht took Khun-Anup's **donkeys** when one of them ate some corn in the evil overseer's field. Khun-Anup went to the Hall of Justice to plead his case. His **eloquence** moved the High Steward, **Meruitensa**. However, the judges dismissed his case. For **nine** straight days, he argued his case until he finally received **justice**.

 Paris, a prince of Troy, stole **Helen** from her husband. A shipwreck brought them to Egypt, where she sought protection from the pharaoh, **Seti II**. She hid in the Temple of **Hathor** with the pharaoh's daughter **Tausret**. The god Thoth separated her **Ka** from her body, and her spirit went to Troy with Paris while her body stayed in Egypt. She was safe until the new pharaoh, **Ramesses III**, wanted to marry her. Fortunately, her husband arrived, the victim of another **shipwreck**, and she was able to escape with him.

Chapter 10 Answers

Word Search

```
A O H Q L X A S F Y H O R U S
S K H E P R I P R E A M M I T
E K Q K V E D H R I Q C V T O
T Z S F H R P I G O U I K V A
P H A T H U L N D S Y A P R O
A R H Z N A F X U I Y P D R P
U A I Y A L T U A R C E K H K
R J A A R M I H T I E P B O S
U Z B U D W A I O S Y I A D D
S C N E W A M N N R Y Q B O J
O V D I N X N K K E U R J P E
D P W M S B I U D H U G P I D
T H O T H I E Y B H T E G S I
M A A T J T S N M I X J T M D
M L E O Y B R E Y S S I O P W
```

Zazamankh	Rhodopis	Benben	Isis
Hathor	Osiris	Khepri	Duat
Anubis	Khufu	Sphinx	Auru
Horus	Thoth	Ammit	Set
Djedi	Maat	Apep	Ra

Image source[64]

Here's another book by Enthralling History that you might like

Free limited time bonus

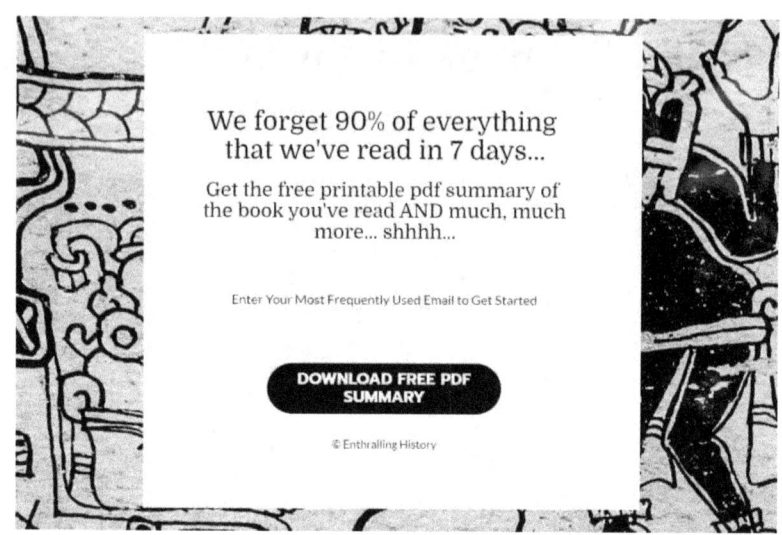

Stop for a moment. We have a free bonus set up for you. The problem is this: we forget 90% of everything that we read after 7 days. Crazy fact, right? Here's the solution: we've created a printable, 1-page pdf summary for this book that you're reading now. All you have to do to get your free pdf summary is to go to the following website: https://livetolearn.lpages.co/enthrallinghistory/

Or, Scan the QR code!

Once you do, it will be intuitive. Enjoy, and thank you!

Bibliography

Assmann, Jan. *The Search for God in Ancient Egypt.* Translated by David Lorton. Ithaca: Cornell University Press, 2001.

Conman, Joanne. "It's About Time: Ancient Egyptian Cosmology." *Studien Zur Altägyptischen Kultur* 31 (2003): 33-71. http://www.jstor.org/stable/25152883.

David, Rosalie. *Religion and Magic in Ancient Egypt.* London: Penguin Books, 2002.

Dunand, Françoise and Christiane Zivie-Coche. *Gods and Men in Egypt: 3000 BCE to 395 CE.* Translated by David Lorton. Ithaca: Cornell University Press, 2004.

Eusebius. *The Egyptian Chronicle.* Translated by Robert Bedrosian. http://www.attalus.org/armenian/euseb.html

Gardiner, Sir Alan. *Egypt of the Pharaohs.* Oxford: Oxford University Press, 1979.

Graur, Or. "The Ancient Egyptian Personification of the Milky Way as the Sky-Goddess Nut: An Astronomical and Cross-Cultural Analysis." *Journal of Astronomical History and Heritage* 27, no. 1 (2004): 28 - 45.

Hart, George. *Egyptian Myths.* Austin: University of Texas Press, 1990.

O'Connor, David, ed. and Stephen Quirke, ed. *Mysterious Lands: Encounters with Ancient Egypt.* London & New York: Routledge, 2016.

Oden, Robert A. "'The Contendings of Horus and Seth' (Chester Beatty Papyrus No. 1): A Structural Interpretation." History of Religions 18, no. 4 (1979): 352-69. http://www.jstor.org/stable/1062192.

Pinch, Geraldine. *Egyptian Mythology: A Guide to the Gods, Goddesses, and Traditions of Ancient Egypt.* Oxford: Oxford University Press, 2002.

Redford, Donald B. "Egypt and Western Asia in the Old Kingdom." *Journal of the American Research Center in Egypt* 23 (1986): 125-43. https://doi.org/10.2307/40001094.

Shaw, Garry J. *The Egyptian Myths: A Guide to the Ancient Gods and Legends*. London: Thames & Hudson, 2014.

"The Land of the Dead," *The Book of Thoth*. Ancient Egypt: The Mythology. http://www.egyptianmyths.net/mythlanddead.htm.

Wiener, Malcolm H. "Egypt & Time." *Ägypten und Levante / Egypt and the Levant* 16 (2006): 325-39. http://www.jstor.org/stable/23790293.

Image Sources

1 Eternal Space, CC BY-SA 4.0 <https://creativecommons.org/licenses/by-sa/4.0>, via Wikimedia Commons : https://commons.wikimedia.org/wiki/File:Tefnut_(Goddess).png
2 Dendera_Deckenrelief_02.JPG: Olaf Tauschderivative work: JMCC1 (talk)photographe/égyptologue, CC BY 3.0 <https://creativecommons.org/licenses/by/3.0>, via Wikimedia Commons: https://commons.wikimedia.org/wiki/File:L%27Ogdoade_d%27Hermopolis.jpg
3 Metropolitan Museum of Art, CC0, via Wikimedia Commons: https://commons.wikimedia.org/wiki/File:Scarab_finger_rign_with_the_name_of_Maatkare_MET_25.3.193_EGDP021780.jpg
4 Jeff Dahl, CC BY-SA 4.0 <https://creativecommons.org/licenses/by-sa/4.0>, via Wikimedia Commons: https://commons.wikimedia.org/wiki/File:Ptah_standing.svg
5 https://commons.wikimedia.org/wiki/File:Nut1.JPG
6 Eternal Space, CC BY-SA 4.0 <https://creativecommons.org/licenses/by-sa/4.0>, via Wikimedia Commons: https://commons.wikimedia.org/wiki/File:Maat_(Goddess).png
7 https://commons.wikimedia.org/wiki/File:Book_of_Gates_Barque_of_Ra_cropped.jpg
8 https://commons.wikimedia.org/wiki/File:Apep_1.jpg
9 Jeff Dahl, CC BY-SA 4.0 <https://creativecommons.org/licenses/by-sa/4.0>, via Wikimedia Commons: https://commons.wikimedia.org/wiki/File:Re-Horakhty.svg
10 Jon Bodsworth, Copyrighted free use, via Wikimedia Commons: https://commons.wikimedia.org/wiki/File:Akhenaten_statue.jpg
11 Djehouty, CC BY-SA 4.0 <https://creativecommons.org/licenses/by-sa/4.0>, via

Wikimedia Commons: https://commons.wikimedia.org/wiki/File:Respaldo_del_trono_de_oro_de_Tutankam%C3%B3n.jpg

12 https://commons.wikimedia.org/wiki/File:Cheprer.JPG

13 Louvre Museum, CC BY-SA 2.0 FR <https://creativecommons.org/licenses/by-sa/2.0/fr/deed.en>, via Wikimedia Commons: https://commons.wikimedia.org/wiki/File:Mnevis-E_6857-IMG_7967.JPG

14 https://commons.wikimedia.org/wiki/File:Fenix_bennu.jpg

15 HarJIT. Derived from files from Rawpixel, Jeff Dahl, Finn Bjørklid and RootOfAllLight., CC BY-SA 4.0 <https://creativecommons.org/licenses/by-sa/4.0>, via Wikimedia Commons: https://commons.wikimedia.org/wiki/File:Central_Hypocephalus_Scene.svg

16 Metropolitan Museum of Art, CC0, via Wikimedia Commons: https://commons.wikimedia.org/wiki/File:The_King_with_Isis,_Tomb_of_Haremhab_MET_DP276167.jpg

17 Eternal Space, CC BY-SA 4.0 <https://creativecommons.org/licenses/by-sa/4.0>, via Wikimedia Commons: https://commons.wikimedia.org/wiki/File:Set_(God).png

18 Photo zoomed in. Metropolitan Museum of Art, CC BY-SA 2.5 <https://creativecommons.org/licenses/by-sa/2.5>, via Wikimedia Commons: https://commons.wikimedia.org/wiki/File:Nephthys-FromAPaintedShroud_MetropolitanMuseumOfArt.png

19 Photo zoomed in. Source: Quibell,1898, pl. 13, CC BY-SA 4.0 <https://creativecommons.org/licenses/by-sa/4.0>, via Wikimedia Commons: https://commons.wikimedia.org/wiki/File:Narmer_Palette_recto.svg

20 https://commons.wikimedia.org/wiki/File:Horus.jpg

21 Gunawan Kartapranata, CC BY-SA 3.0 <https://creativecommons.org/licenses/by-sa/3.0>, via Wikimedia Commons: https://commons.wikimedia.org/wiki/File:Bastet.svg

22 https://commons.wikimedia.org/wiki/File:Egyptian_-_Squatting_Thoth_Baboon_-_Walters_542143_-_Right.jpg

23 Jeff Dahl, CC BY-SA 4.0 <https://creativecommons.org/licenses/by-sa/4.0>, via Wikimedia Commons: https://commons.wikimedia.org/wiki/File:Taweret.svg

24 Eternal Space, CC BY-SA 4.0 <https://creativecommons.org/licenses/by-sa/4.0>, via Wikimedia Commons: https://commons.wikimedia.org/wiki/File:Hapi_(God).png

25 https://commons.wikimedia.org/wiki/File:Sovk_(Suchus,_Cronos,_Satrune),_N372.2.jpg

26 https://commons.wikimedia.org/wiki/File:Osiris_2.jpg

27 Photo zoomed in. Source: Metropolitan Museum of Art, CC0, via Wikimedia Commons: https://commons.wikimedia.org/wiki/File:Isis_with_Horus_MET_DP238574.jpg

28 Eternal Space, CC BY-SA 4.0 <https://creativecommons.org/licenses/by-sa/4.0>, via Wikimedia Commons: https://commons.wikimedia.org/wiki/File:Horus_(God).png

29 Photo zoomed in. Source: Buchsweiler, CC BY-SA 3.0 <https://creativecommons.org/licenses/by-sa/3.0>, via Wikimedia Commons: https://commons.wikimedia.org/wiki/File:Enneade.jpg

30 Eb.hoop, CC BY-SA 3.0 <https://creativecommons.org/licenses/by-sa/3.0>, via Wikimedia Commons: https://commons.wikimedia.org/wiki/File:MetternichStela.jpg

31 https://commons.wikimedia.org/wiki/File:Egyptian_-_Figure_of_Isis-Serget_as_Scorpion_-_Walters_54546_-_Side_A_(cropped).jpg

32 Jl FilpoC, CC BY-SA 4.0 <https://creativecommons.org/licenses/by-sa/4.0>, via Wikimedia Commons: https://commons.wikimedia.org/wiki/File:Dibujo_del_dios_Thoth,_British_Museum.jpg

33 https://commons.wikimedia.org/wiki/File:01927_3_1_0_17_2860_164325_Zabytki_z_wyposa%C5%BCenia_grobowca_faraona_Tutanchamona_z_Egiptu,_Izis.jpg

34 https://commons.wikimedia.org/wiki/File:Egyptian_-_Isis_Nursing_Harpocrates_-_Walters_481526_-_Detail_A.jpg

35 Photo zoomed in. https://commons.wikimedia.org/wiki/File:Opening_of_the_mouth_ceremony.jpg

36 https://commons.wikimedia.org/wiki/File:Anubis_attending_the_mummy_of_Sennedjem.jpg

37 Photo zoomed in, https://commons.wikimedia.org/wiki/File:Medjed_Bodmer_100.jpg

38 Photo zoomed in. https://commons.wikimedia.org/wiki/File:Book_of_the_Dead_of_Hunefer_sheet_3.jpg

39 Photo zoomed in. https://commons.wikimedia.org/wiki/File:Book_of_the_Dead_of_Hunefer_sheet_3.jpg

40 Photo zoomed in. Source: Museo Egizio, CC BY 4.0 <https://creativecommons.org/licenses/by/4.0>, via Wikimedia Commons: https://commons.wikimedia.org/wiki/File:Shabti_of_Amenhotep,_faience_-_Museo_Egizio,_Turin_C_2561_p02.jpg

41 Photo zoomed in. Source: Metropolitan Museum of Art, CC0, via Wikimedia Commons: https://commons.wikimedia.org/wiki/File:The_Singer_of_Amun_Nany%27s_Funerary_Papyrus_MET_DT11633.jpg

42 https://crosswordlabs.com/view/egyptian-mythology-the-underworld

43 Photo zoomed in. Source: Olaf Tausch, CC BY 3.0 <https://creativecommons.org/licenses/by/3.0>, via Wikimedia Commons: https://commons.wikimedia.org/wiki/File:Luxor_Museum_Statuenkopf_Echnaton_01.jpg

44 Jean-Pierre Dalbéra, CC BY 2.0 <https://creativecommons.org/licenses/by/2.0>, via Wikimedia Commons: ttps://commons.wikimedia.org/wiki/File:T%C3%AAte_de_Tout%C3%A2nkhamon_enfant_(mus%C3%A9e_du_Caire_Egypte).jpg

45 https://commons.wikimedia.org/wiki/File:Maia_and_tut.gif

46 https://commons.wikimedia.org/wiki/File:Tutankhamun_tomb_photographs_4_326.jpg

47 en:User:MykReeve, CC BY-SA 3.0 <http://creativecommons.org/licenses/by-sa/3.0/>, via Wikimedia Commons: https://commons.wikimedia.org/wiki/File:Tutanchamun_Maske.jpg

48 Hatty321, CC BY 2.0 <https://creativecommons.org/licenses/by/2.0>, via Wikimedia Commons: https://commons.wikimedia.org/wiki/File:Egyptian_sculpture_on_Avenue_of_Sphinxes_(45765061544).jpg

49 Photo zoomed in. Source: Osama Shukir Muhammed Amin FRCP(Glasg), CC BY-SA 4.0 <https://creativecommons.org/licenses/by-sa/4.0>, via Wikimedia Commons: https://commons.wikimedia.org/wiki/File:Bracer_of_Pharaoh_Thutmose_IV._From_Amarna,_House_P_48.1,_Egypt._1397-1388_BCE._Neues_Museum.jpg

50 Petar Milošević, CC BY-SA 4.0 <https://creativecommons.org/licenses/by-sa/4.0>, via Wikimedia Commons: https://commons.wikimedia.org/wiki/File:Great_Sphinx_of_Giza_(%D8%A3%D8%A8%D9%88_%D8%A7%D9%84%D9%87%D9%88%D9%84).jpg.

51 Chanel Wheeler, CC BY-SA 2.0 <https://creativecommons.org/licenses/by-sa/2.0>, via Wikimedia Commons: https://commons.wikimedia.org/wiki/File:Great_Sphinx_with_Stelae.jpg

52 Gérard Ducher (Néfermaât), CC BY-SA 2.5 <https://creativecommons.org/licenses/by-sa/2.5>, via Wikimedia Commons: https://commons.wikimedia.org/wiki/File:GD-EG-Alex-Mus%C3%A9eNat074.JPG

53 Photo zoomed in. https://commons.wikimedia.org/wiki/File:Narmer_Palette_serpopard_side.jpg

54 Osama Shukir Muhammed Amin FRCP(Glasg), CC BY-SA 4.0 <https://creativecommons.org/licenses/by-sa/4.0>, via Wikimedia Commons: https://commons.wikimedia.org/wiki/File:Pharaoh_Seti_I,_detail_of_a_wall_painting_from_the_Tomb_of_Seti_I_at_the_Valley_of_the_Kings,_Western_Thebes,_Egypt._Neues_Museum.jpg

55 Nina M. Davies, CC0, via Wikimedia Commons: https://commons.wikimedia.org/wiki/File:Laden_Donkeys_and_Ploughing,_Tomb_of_Djar_MET_31.6.2_EGDP013009.jpg

56 Museo Egizio, CC BY 2.5 <https://creativecommons.org/licenses/by/2.5>, via Wikimedia Commons:

https://commons.wikimedia.org/wiki/File:Statue_of_Seti_II,_sandstone_-_Museo_Egizio_Turin_C_1383_p02.jpg

57 Yair Haklai, CC BY-SA 3.0 <https://creativecommons.org/licenses/by-sa/3.0>, via Wikimedia Commons; https://commons.wikimedia.org/wiki/File:Antonio_Canova-Helen_of_Troy-Victoria_and_Albert_Museum.jpg

58 Émile Prisse d'Avennes (1807-1879), CC BY 4.0 <https://creativecommons.org/licenses/by/4.0>, via Wikimedia Commons: https://commons.wikimedia.org/wiki/File:Queen_Tausret_%C3%89mile_Prisse_d%27Avennes.jpg

59 Mary Harrsch, CC BY-SA 4.0 <https://creativecommons.org/licenses/by-sa/4.0>, via Wikimedia Commons: https://commons.wikimedia.org/wiki/File:Menelaus_bearing_the_corpse_of_Patroclus._Marble,_Flavian_Era_(1st_century_CE)_Roman_copy_after_a_Hellenistic_original_of_the_3rd_century_BCE_MH_04.jpg

60 Photo zoomed in. Source: Louvre Museum, CC BY-SA 2.0 FR <https://creativecommons.org/licenses/by-sa/2.0/fr/deed.en>, via Wikimedia Commons: https://commons.wikimedia.org/wiki/File:Hetepi_chief_magician-E_123-IMG_8049-gradient.jpg

61 Vassil, CC0, via Wikimedia Commons: https://commons.wikimedia.org/wiki/File:Collier_Lotus_Neues_Museum_26042018.jpg

62 Osama Shukir Muhammed Amin FRCP(Glasg), CC BY-SA 4.0 <https://creativecommons.org/licenses/by-sa/4.0>, via Wikimedia Commons: https://commons.wikimedia.org/wiki/File:Head_of_Amasis_II,_c._550_BCE._From_Egypt._Neues_Museum,_Berlin,_Germany.jpg

63 https://www.education.com/

64 https://www.education.com/

www.ingramcontent.com/pod-product-compliance
Lightning Source LLC
Chambersburg PA
CBHW070334010526
44107CB00004B/505